Logistics Competencies, Skills, and Training

WORLD BANK STUDY

Logistics Competencies, Skills, and Training

A Global Overview

Alan McKinnon, Christoph Flöthmann, Kai Hoberg, and Christina Busch

WORLD BANK GROUP

Contents

Map

Tables

Acknowledgments

This report has been commissioned by the World Bank's Global Trade Team at the Trade and Competitiveness Global Practice, under the guidance of Jose Guilherme Reis (practice manager). The report was prepared by Alan C. McKinnon, Christoph Flöthmann, and Kai Hoberg at the Kühne Logistics University in Hamburg, Germany, with additions from Christina Busch and Jean-François Arvis at the World Bank.

The project leaders were Christina Busch and Jean-François Arvis. Thomas Farole and Virginia Tanase were peer reviewers for the project concept note. Robin Carruthers, Claire Hollweg, and Sanda Liepina were peer reviewers for the report.

The authors and project leaders can be reached at Alan.McKinnon@the -klu.org, Christoph.Floethmann@the-klu.org, Kai.Hoberg@the-klu.org, and cbusch@worldbank.org.

About the Authors

Alan McKinnon is professor of logistics in the Kühne Logistics University in Hamburg. He was founder and director of the Logistics Research Centre at Heriot-Watt University, Edinburgh, until January 2012 and is now a professor emeritus of this university. He holds or has held visiting professorships in China, Malaysia, South Africa, Sweden, and the United Kingdom A graduate of the universities of Aberdeen, British Columbia, and London, he has been researching and teaching in freight transport/logistics for over 35 years and has published extensively in journals and books on many different aspects of the subject. Much of his recent research has focused on the links between logistics and climate change. He was a lead author of the transport chapter in the latest Assessment Report of the Intergovernmental Panel on Climate Change. McKinnon has been an adviser to several governments, parliamentary committees, and international organizations including the Organisation for Economic Co-operation and Development, World Bank, and United Nations. He was chairman of the World Economic Forum's Logistics and Supply Chain Council and is currently a member of its Council on the Future of Mobility. He was a member of the European Commission's High Level Group on Logistics, and, until recently, was chairman of the Transport Advisory Group of the EU Horizon 2020 research program. He is Fellow of the Chartered Institute of Logistics and Transport and a recipient of its highest distinction, the Sir Robert Lawrence Award. In 2015 he was appointed a Fellow of the European Logistics Association.

Christoph Flöthmann is a PhD candidate in supply chain management (SCM) at Kühne Logistics University and Copenhagen Business School. Beforehand, he graduated with a diploma degree (MSc-equivalent) in business administration with majors in SCM and management science, finance and transport economics, from the University of Cologne. Flöthmann's research focuses on the intersection of SCM and human resource management. In particular, his empirical research is concerned with the backgrounds, competencies, and contributions of people managing supply chains. His research has been published in the *Journal of Business Logistics, Supply Chain Management Review*, and *Logistik Heute* (German). Before starting his academic career, he gained practical experience at OSCAR Consulting GmbH, Bayer MaterialScience AG, and DB Schenker AG in Germany and Indonesia.

Kai Hoberg has been an associate professor of supply chain and operations strategy at the Kühne Logistics University, Hamburg, since May 2012. He was an assistant professor of supply chain management at the University of Cologne, Germany, and received his PhD from Münster University, Germany. Before returning to academia, Hoberg worked as a strategy consultant and project manager in the operations practice of Booz & Company. During his academic career he has conducted research at various universities, for example, Cornell University, Israel Institute of Technology, National University of Singapore, and University of Oxford. Hoberg's research focuses on strategic and data-driven topics in logistics and supply chain management. He publishes in highly ranked academic journals like the *Journal of Operations Management, Production and Operations Management,* and *Journal of Business Logistics.* Hoberg currently supervises four PhD students and cooperates with companies like Procter & Gamble, McKinsey & Company, and Jungheinrich.

Christina Busch is an economist at the World Bank Group in Washington, DC. She is part of the Global Trade Team within the Trade and Competitiveness Global Practice. Busch joined the World Bank in 2012 and has worked with the Trade Logistics and Connectivity team since 2013. She has contributed to analytical, advisory, and lending activities in the areas of trade logistics, regional integration, connectivity, and trade facilitation. Busch is a co-author of the World Bank's 2014 and 2016 Logistics Performance Index. Before joining the World Bank Group, Busch worked in the economic policy program of the Bertelsmann Foundation in Germany. Previously, she served as director of programs at the Friedrich Naumann Foundation in Washington, DC. Christina holds an MSc degree in economics (Diplom-Volkswirtin) from Humboldt-Universitaet zu Berlin and a master of public administration degree from Columbia University. She is currently pursuing a PhD in economics at Technische Universität Berlin, Germany.

Executive Summary

Efficient supply chains are critical to economic development, trade integration and competitiveness. Logistics services are typically provided by a private logistics company to a retail or industrial firm. The quality and efficiency of these services heavily depend on economy-wide features, including government interventions, which are typically referred to as logistics performance, following the World Bank Logistics Performance Index (LPI). Countries experience large differences in their logistics performance, and lower quality of service negatively impacts production and international trade.

Public interventions and private public dialogue play an important role in enhancing performance and in establishing sustainable supply chain connections both internationally and domestically. Government policies include the soft and hard infrastructure of trade and commerce, trade facilitation initiatives, and regulation. Government and international agencies have traditionally paid more attention to infrastructure and trade facilitation than to fostering the development of quality services and a skilled workforce.

Logistics at the operational level is a labor-intensive industry with many blue collar workers (e.g., truck drivers, warehouse operators) and administrative clerks. How well these employees are qualified, trained and retained is a major factor of logistics performance. Yet this factor is often overlooked or taken for granted. It depends not only on HR policies of specific companies but also on national initiatives to educate and train for occupations in the sector. This report attempts at filling this gap in the knowledge of skills and competencies, and solutions to upgrade them. It expands observations made in the World Bank's 2016 LPI report.

This report has been prepared by the World Bank and its research partners at the Kühne Logistics University (KLU). It is the first of its kind to look at skills and competencies in logistics globally. It sheds light on the present state of training, recruitment and retention in logistics and supply chain management. It evaluates the perceived challenges of finding and retaining qualified employees across countries and across job categories. The project compares the logistics skills and training situations in developing markets in Africa, South America and Asia with those of more developed countries in Europe and North America. It identifies examples of good practices and institutions to "upskill" the logistics sectors. Finally, one of this study's main outputs is guidance to governments and stakeholders of developing countries on how to upgrade logistics skills and training capabilities.

The study builds on multiple sources. An online survey of logistics companies worldwide was carried out. In addition, data from the LPI 2016 survey was used. 36 interviews of experts in logistics education and training in all major world regions were conducted. Case studies and examples have been developed to examine the needs and initiatives taken in specific sectors. Detailed attention has been given to the trucking sector given its social and environmental footprint in most developing countries. The report also depicts examples of country initiatives involving government, stakeholders in the logistics community, educational institutions, professional associations and recruitment and training agencies. Finally the report identifies reference resources which can be used as part of national "upskilling" initiatives.

There is no universal standardized taxonomy of logistics activities. For the purpose of this study, the following broad occupational levels are distinguished: (a) operational or blue-collar workers, (b) administrative staff, (c) logistics supervisors, and (d) supply chain managers. These occupational levels include different types of jobs depending on the nature of service or facility.

Key Findings

Both the LPI survey and the survey carried out for this study show a general perception across the logistics sector that qualified logistics-related labor is in short supply on all occupational levels in both developed and developing countries. Shortages range from a lack of truck drivers to problems in filling senior supply chain management positions. Respondents in developing countries point to the supervisory level for the most severe perceived skills shortage (figure ES.1). In developed countries skill shortages were perceived at all levels, but at a much lower level. The survey and other sources suggest that this problem is likely to remain the same or worsen over the next five years.

Backing these observations with "hard" market data would have gone beyond the ambition of this report. Employment and wage statistics are typically not available in developing countries with the expected level of sectoral and occupational details. Yet domestic studies in some countries such as China, India, the United States, the United Kingdom, Vietnam, and the Republic of Korea have reported that businesses are having difficulty recruiting staff with the required skills in logistics/supply chain management.

There is an expert consensus on the reasons for the perceived shortage. In all countries, the logistics sector suffers from low prestige and status of operational logistics workers in many cultures and societies. It offers low salary levels compared to other sectors, leading to an inferior position in the "war for talent". Developing countries face a limited supply of skilled labor, even though countries may suffer from high levels of unemployment. The study

Figure ES.1 Evidence from the 2016 LPI

Respondents indicating "low" or "very low" availability of qualified personnel in the respective employee groups, by LPI Quintile

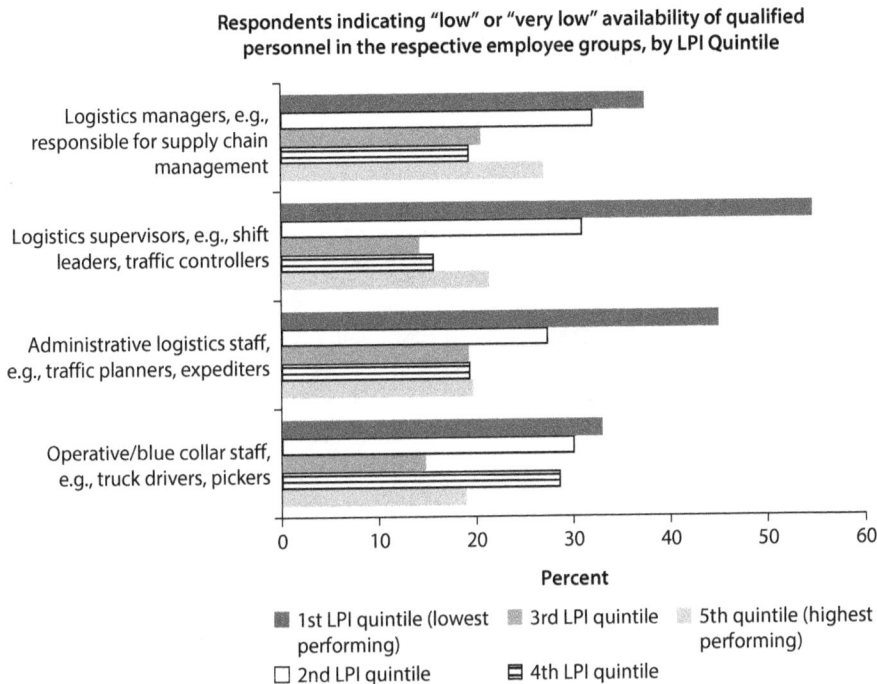

1st LPI quintile (lowest performing)
2nd LPI quintile
3rd LPI quintile
4th LPI quintile
5th quintile (highest performing)

Source: Arvis et al. 2016.

observes a lack of vocational school preparation for logistics jobs. Logistics developments, particularly in IT, demand new competencies that the existing workforce does not possess. This form of market failure disproportionally impacts the young, who typically form an untapped reservoir of apprentices in some occupations (e.g., trucking). The reasons for shortages of blue-collar workers in developed economies are partly similar, such as lack of attractiveness, and are partly tied to cultural aspects and the ageing demographic structure of the logistics workforce.

Upskilling and Retaining the Labor Force

The report highlights the need for a major expansion of logistics training and skills development initiatives in developing countries. Developing regions are lagging behind developed countries in terms of training budgets, course content, and quality of the educational experience and sources of training. Often, training—if offered at all—is limited to short-term, on-the-job training provided by colleagues during daily operations (figure ES.2).

The study describes the roles that the various stakeholder groups can play in the education, training and development of logistics employees, individually and collectively, to upgrade their logistics skill levels. Beyond companies and their employees, other stakeholders such as logistics associations, higher educational

Figure ES.2 Sources of Training

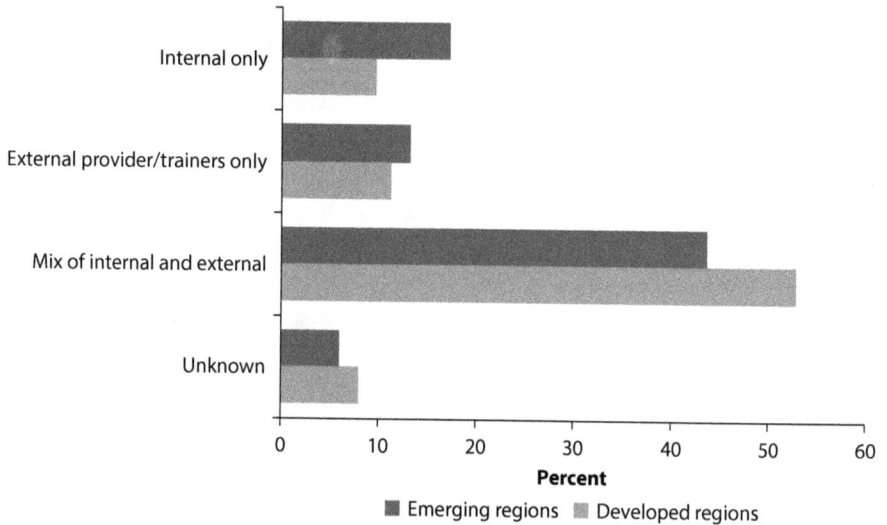

institutes and vocational training institutions have a mutual interest in this effort. The report outlines best practices in competence development that are particularly relevant for developing regions. For instance, training initiatives for the current workforce are facilitated using off-the shelf resources and competencies provided by global reference organizations. FIATA, the global association of freight forwarders, or the International Road Union (for trucking companies) have established training programs or train-the-trainer schemes. These could be deployed even more widely.

Fewer resources exist for the education of potential employees. The report outlines best practices in competence development that are particularly relevant for developing regions. It also proposes training initiatives that can be implemented even on tight budgets and at low maturity levels in the educational and logistics sectors:

- International branch campuses of established Western universities with a strong background in logistics. GeorgiaTech and the Massachusetts Institute of Technology have opened several satellites in emerging economies in Latin America and East Asia. German and Dutch Technical Universities also have established cooperations in logistics globally.
- Updating and adjustment of current university curricula, which could involve international expertise from leading global institutions.
- Multiple stakeholder collaboration such as "dual education" and apprenticeships (e.g., Germany, Austria), which could help create job opportunities for the young.
- Experimental and blended learning approaches, tailored to the needs of the sector.

Expert panels and surveys have emphasized the centrality of human resources management. Recruitment and retention strategies should complement investment in skills. Otherwise the sector might be trapped in a vicious circle where high turnover makes it difficult to "upskill". Companies in the sector must improve their HR policies and strive to retain key employees by offering inter alia:

- Transparent career paths
- Appealing working environments
- Investment in the development of the workforce (training programs at the company level)

In developing countries, support provided by institutions such as the World Bank could include components helping companies enhance their HR strategies.

Quality of recruitment and retention is also a question of image, which in the case of logistics is often poor. Collectively the logistics sector could invest in promoting the image of its professional opportunities, targeting especially the younger professionals. The upsides of a career in logistics must be emphasized: they include internationality, working in intercultural teams, stimulating working environments, mobility, key contribution to the economy and general welfare, and involvement in technological innovation.

The Role of Public Sector Initiatives

Government agencies can play a role in enhancing competencies and skills in the logistics sectors. Hiring employees is done by private companies and training them is largely a private responsibility, too. Nevertheless, governments play an important role either directly (e.g., via regulation or provision of training), or by facilitating private initiatives. Public interventions that leverage logistics competence include the following:

- Provision of education or training by public institutions or financial support to training
- Education policy and development of curricula
- Advocacy, public private dialogue and multi-stakeholder collaboration
- Regulation of freight and logistics services, as certain activities are specifically regulated, including customs brokerage or trucking
- Setting and harmonizing competence standards applicable to different jobs
- Leading by example: raising skills levels in state-owned logistics enterprises (typically ports and railways)
- Investing in human capital as a component of the development of logistics and freight infrastructure

Finally, the study proposes a short guide for policy makers and international organizations intervening to support logistics improvements. It consists of a logistics competence maturity matrix that classifies countries into three categories based on their LPI competence index (basic, intermediate or advanced). The matrix includes summary guidance for (a) a national assessment of skills and competencies and (b) the priority areas of interventions upgrading logistics skill levels, depending on the category of countries. As part of its country work, the World Bank has recently begun offering a more comprehensive assessment of skills and competencies at the national level.

Abbreviations

3PL	third-party logistics service providers
AILOG	Associazione Italiana di Logistica e di Supply Chain Management (Italy)
APICS	Association for Operations Management
ATI	Accredited Training Institutes
BLM	business, logistics, and managerial
BVL	Bundesvereinigung Logistik (Germany)
CEL	Centro Español de Logística
CILT	Chartered Institute of Logistics and Transport
CLI	Center for Latin American Logistics Innovation
CNT	National Confederation of Transport (Brazil)
CPC	certificate of professional competence
CPD	continuing professional development
CSCMP	Council of Supply Chain Management Professionals
CSCP	certified supply chain professional
CTL	Center for Transportation and Logistics
DB	Deutsche Bahn
ELA	European Logistics Association
FIATA	International Federation of Freight Forwarding Associations
GAVI	Global Alliance for Vaccines and Immunization
GCLOG	Graduate Certificate in Logistics and Supply Chain Management (MIT)
GUtech	German University of Technology (Oman)
HGV	heavy goods vehicle
HLA	Humanitarian Logistics Association
HR	human resources
HRM	human resources management
IAMM	Indian Association of Material Management
ICT	information and communication technology
ILO	International Labour Organization

INALOG	Instituto Nacional de Logística (Uruguay)
IRU	International Road Union
ISM	Institute for Supply Chain Management
IT	information technology
KLU	Kühne Logistics University
LATAM	Latin America
LINCS	Leveraging, Integrating, Networking, Coordinating Supplies Program (United States)
LPI	Logistics Performance Index
MGCM	French training agency for logistics and supply chain management
MISI	Malaysia Institute for Supply Chain Innovation
MIT	Massachusetts Institute of Technology
NGO	nongovernmental organization
NHVR	National Heavy Vehicle Regulator Initiative (Australia)
NSDC	National Skills Development Corporation (India)
PPP	public-private partnerships
PtD	People that Deliver
PTL	Polish Supply Management Leaders (industry association)
RWTH	Rheinisch-Westfälische Technische Hochschule (Aachen, Germany)
SCM	supply chain management
SETA	Skills Education Training Authority (South Africa)
SMEs	small and medium enterprises
STEP	Strategic Training Executive Program
TCI	Transport Corporation of India
TETA	Transport Education and Training Authority (South Africa)
TLI	The Logistics Institute
UAE	United Arab Emirates
VP	vice president
WTD	Working Time Directive

CHAPTER 1

Introduction

Background

Logistics has been a major growth sector in the world economy in terms of levels of activity and expenditure for many decades. In addition to being an important sector in its own right, logistics strongly influences the economic performance of other industries and the countries in which they are located. Given its critical importance to economic development and social welfare, logistics must be adequately resourced—in the physical sense and in terms of human resources. Despite extensive mechanization and automation, logistics at the operational level intrinsically remains a people business. This makes the logistics performance of companies and countries highly dependent on the quantity and quality of the workforce.

The policy focus and national business dialogues have so far emphasized infrastructure, investment climate, or trade facilitation. Increasingly, human resources, competencies and skills are a collective concern, too. Studies in countries such as China, India, the United States, the United Kingdom, Vietnam, and the Republic of Korea have reported that businesses are having difficulty recruiting staff with the required skills in logistics/supply chain management. These skills shortages range from a lack of truck drivers to problems in filling senior supply chain management (SCM) positions. Why do many employed logistics staff lack the necessary competencies to adequately perform the tasks they are assigned? This could reflect the competence of the people attracted into the industry, the level of training they receive and the way they are managed and motivated. The logistics sector's recruitment potential is often constrained by its relatively poor image. Career planning can also be deficient, with the result that some high-caliber operatives and managers abandon logistics for other roles.

Measuring Logistics Competence in the Logistics Performance Index

Macro-level evidence of the problem can be found in the World Bank's bi-annual Logistics Performance Index (LPI) report. This survey-based index was established to help countries identify the challenges and opportunities they face in the field of trade logistics and what they can do to improve their logistical performance. The LPI 2014 survey compares the performance of 160 countries (Arvis et al. 2014). The respondents assess the six key components of logistics performance listed in box 1.1. The fourth criterion, the quality of logistics in a country and its competence to provide it, is the one most closely related to this study.

There is a reasonably close relationship between aggregate LPI scores and GDP per capita values. A simple regression analysis was done to assess whether (logarithmic) GDP per capita is a good predictor of logistics quality/competence scores, using LPI 2014 data. As figure 1.1 shows, developed countries with high GDPs per capita are ranked higher than developing countries in their LPI quality & competence score. But GDP per capita is not a perfect predictor. Green and red labels have been used in figure 1.1 to show how countries can have much higher or lower logistics competence scores than their GDP per capita would suggest.

This diagram also shows that over- and underperformers are present in all income groups, that is, low-income, middle-income, and high-income countries. The statistical analysis indicates that countries can reach higher levels of logistics competence than their economic output per capita predicts. This fact should serve as a strong motivation for the various stakeholder groups (e.g., governments, logistics companies and associations) in under-performing countries to upskill their workforce. In trying to upgrade its logistics, a country would be well advised to expand logistics skills and training initiatives. It would also benefit from external guidance on how to devise and implement such initiatives, partly on the basis of experience in countries such as the United Kingdom and Germany, which have a good track record of upgrading and professionalizing their logistics workforce.

Figure 1.1 LPI 2014 "Logistics Quality & Competence" Score, Over- and Underperformers

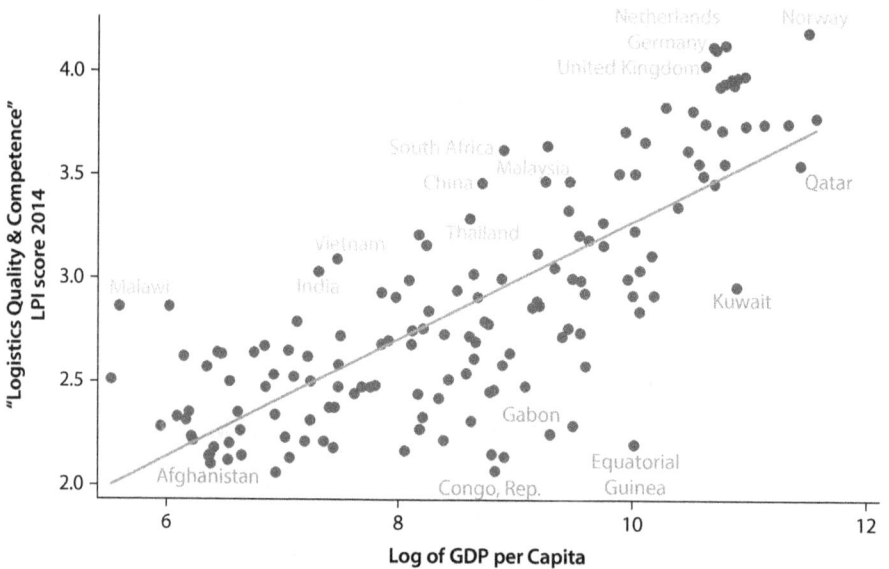

Box 1.1 Criteria Used in the Logistics Performance Index (LPI) Survey

1. Efficiency of customs and border clearance
2. Quality of trade and transport infrastructure
3. Ease of arranging competitively priced shipments
4. Competence and quality of logistics services—primarily in trucking, forwarding and customs brokerage
5. Ability to track and trace consignments
6. Timeliness—frequency with which shipments reach consignees within scheduled or expected delivery times

---

To supplement the analysis of the World Bank/KLU report, the 2016 LPI edition for the first time included a question on logistics skills and competencies. Respondents were asked to indicate the availability (from "very high" to "very low") of qualified personnel for four groups of logistics personnel:

1. Operative staff, for example, truck drivers or warehouse pickers
2. Administrative staff, for example, traffic planners, expediters or warehouse clerks
3. Logistics supervisors, for example, warehouse shift leaders or traffic controllers
4. Logistics managers, for example, those responsible for transport, warehousing operations or SCM.

Responses to the survey confirm a global perception of scarcity of adequately qualified personnel at all four occupational levels in both developed and developing countries, but particularly in the countries that form the bottom quintile in the LPI (figure 1.2). In those countries, the shortage of logistics staff in the "mid tiers", that is, administrative staff and supervisors, is most acute. A similar picture emerges in the second-lowest LPI quintile, where the share of low or very low availability was rated at around a third for all four occupational levels. The problem of skills shortages is less acute but equally present in the third, fourth and fifth LPI quintile.

When broken down by geographic region, Latin America and the Caribbean emerges as the region with the highest skills gap across all employee groups (figure 1.3). A full 43 percent of respondents for instance indicated that the availability of logistics managers, that is, those with the most sophisticated responsibilities, was either "low" or "very low". Yet also for each of the three remaining employee groups (operative, administrative and supervisory), about a third of respondents indicated low or very low availability of staff.

Comparatively high skills deficits of between 20 percent and 30 percent at all job levels were reported in South Asia and Sub-Saharan Africa. The picture is more nuanced in East Asia and Pacific, were shortages of administrative and managerial staff were more acute than those of operative and supervisory staff. In the Middle East and North Africa, the low level of staff

Figure 1.2 Availability of Qualified Personnel by Employee Group and LPI Quintile

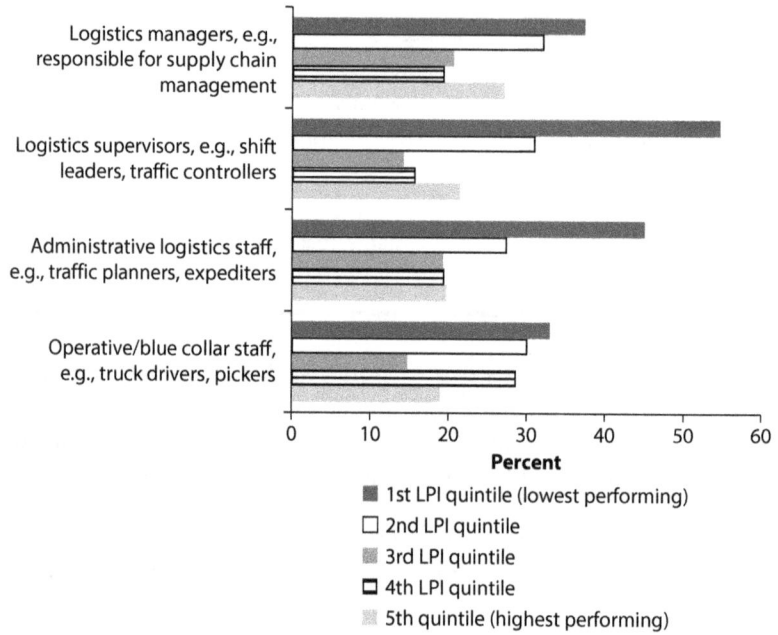

Source: Logistics Performance Index 2016.

Figure 1.3 Availability of Qualified Personnel by Region

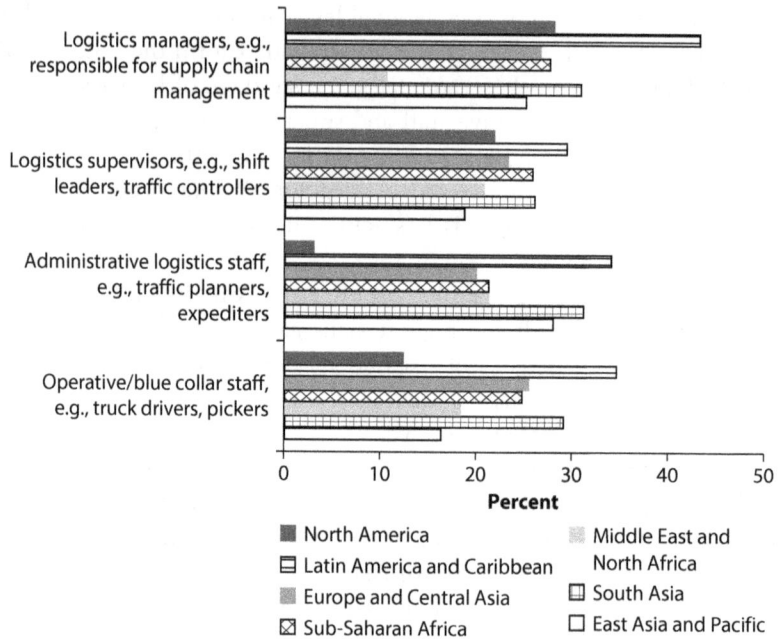

Source: Logistics Performance Index 2016.

shortage at the managerial level (11 percent) vs. the other levels (around 20 percent each) stands out. This could be a favorable outcome of higher education programs (B.Sc. and M.Sc.) in logistics and SCM that were introduced in the region over the past decade. Morocco could serve as an example of a country that owing to those programs does not see a severe shortage of managerial staff. However, difficulties in finding workers on lower sophistication levels, for example, truck drivers and warehouse pickers, are still pertinent in the country.

Scope and Objectives of the Report

The report builds on this observations and provides the first global overview of skills and competencies in logistics. Thus it provides perception survey data on the current supply of and demand for qualified logistics personnel across the four occupational levels and around the globe. Furthermore, it sheds light on the current state of training, recruitment, retention and related challenges in the logistics/SCM field.

This report has four objectives:

1. Review the nature (occupational level and geographical patterns) of the perceived shortages of qualified logistics personnel around the world, particularly in developing economies.
2. Review the current practices of training and skill development in developing regions and suggest improvements based on best practice examples.
3. Review the recruitment and retention strategies for logistics companies that are applicable around the globe. Potential challenges for human resources management (HRM) in the logistics sector over the next five years are also discussed.
4. Provide guidance for public sector on helping upgrade the logistics workforce and identify a set of actions that governmental agencies can take.

Conceptual Framework

The report builds on several concepts which will be referred to throughout the document.

Definition of logistics: Includes the range of activities related to the movement, storage and handling of goods and related information and communication technology (ICT). It encompasses SCM responsibilities, but excludes employees whose main focus is purchasing, production management or sales. The functional range is defined by the nature of the job rather than the type of business. It is not, therefore, confined to the employees of logistics companies and includes staff performing logistics tasks in the manufacturing and retail/wholesale sectors. In the context of the poorest countries, humanitarian and health logistics play a large role, and these are affected by the skills shortage as well.

Logistics Competencies, Skills, and Training • http://dx.doi.org/10.1596/978-1-4648-1140-1

Labor markets and skills shortage: The ability of a country to meet the labor requirements of logistics/SCM can be defined in terms of both demand and supply. Ideally the demand would be measured in two ways: by the number of personnel required and by their required skill levels, and the supply by the numbers of people being trained and the number of apprentices and graduates entering the sector. Unfortunately this market data is not available, certainly not globally, and rarely so nationally even in advanced economies. For these reasons. In assessing the scale of skills shortages and the level of educational/training support, the report relies on survey data and indirect evidence. These provide qualitative information on the ease of finding and retaining adequate skills in a given country environment. Hereafter, any reference in the report to a shortage refers to the subjective difficulty of finding adequately skilled staff according to requirements of the survey respondents.

Levels of skill and responsibility: In this report, four levels of logistics staff are distinguished: a) operatives b) administrators c) supervisors and d) managers. A mature logistics job market would have an adequate supply of staff at each of these levels. Obviously, each level requires a different set of skills and knowledge. These occupational levels are explained in chapter 3.

Geography: The report takes a global perspective on the availability of logistics skills and the efforts to improve it. Time and resource constraints did not allow us to conduct a comprehensive overview of all countries. Since developing countries tend to get lower scores on the logistics competence criterion, they received much of the attention. Experts from developed countries were surveyed and interviewed as they can act as benchmarks and role models. They are a source of good practice on how to develop logistics/SCM as a career path and profession. A set of best practice examples was compiled that developing countries can adopt to improve their logistics skill bases. The study examines the situation in developed countries partly because they are also experiencing logistics recruitment problems. The report contains a case study of the truck driver shortage, which is currently causing concern in the US and several European countries, and likewise in India. In recent years, migration has helped some countries relieve labor shortages in the logistics sector. For instance, Western Europe heavily depends on truck drivers from Eastern Europe to fill vacant positions. New recruits in Thai warehouses often migrate from the Lao People's Democratic Republic and Myanmar. Therefore, the report considers the contribution that migration can make to the cross-border transfer of logistics skills and competencies.

Stakeholders: There are many stakeholders involved in developing and certifying logistics competencies and generally addressing the problem of labor shortages. Accordingly, experts from several stakeholder groups were interviewed and surveyed (see interview and survey sample overview in chapter 2). By examining the roles of these various stakeholders, the report aims to provide an integrated overview from numerous perspectives.

Report Outline

The report is structured as follows: chapter 2 introduces the methodology implemented in the report and the sources of data and information. Chapter 3 discusses the results of surveys on logistics competence requirements and shortages across all world regions. Chapter 4 includes sector case studies in the trucking industry and humanitarian logistics sectors. Chapter 5 addresses training and skills development, in particular, sources of training, stakeholders and best practices. Chapter 6 sheds light on recruitment and retention strategies. Chapter 7 provides guidance and recommendations for public sector institutions. Chapter 8 presents a logistics competence matrix, a framework that enables stakeholders to self-assess the level of logistics competence in their country and provides a brief overview for possible activities to raise the competence level. Chapter 9 summarizes the report.

Reference

Arvis, J.-F., D. Saslavsky, L. Ojala, B. Shepherd, C. Busch, A. Raj, and T. Naula. 2016. *Connecting to Compete 2016—Trade Logistics in the Global Economy*. The International Bank for Reconstruction and Development/The World Bank.

CHAPTER 2

Methodology and Sources

The report draws on a mix of research methodologies and data sources. The combination of qualitative semi-structured interviews, a quantitative online survey and a comprehensive literature review enables us to study logistics competencies and their development from multiple perspectives.

Semi-structured interviews: 36 telephone/Skype and two face-to-face interviews were carried out with five categories of stakeholders. Map 2.1 shows a map with all countries covered during the interviews. Table 2.1 provides a breakdown by region and examples of job titles and descriptions. Due to a confidentiality agreement, company and personal names are not disclosed. The sample of interviewees included:

1. Distinguished researchers working in the fields of logistics and SCM
2. Representatives of professional logistics institutes including CILT (Chartered Institute of Logistics and Transport, United Kingdom and International), BVL (Bundesvereinigung Logistik, Germany), ELA (European Logistics Association, Europe as a whole), CSCMP (Council of Supply Chain Management Professionals, United States), IAMM (Indian Association of Material Management), APICS (Association for Operations Management), and regional logistics training agencies
3. Representatives of government-sponsored agencies responsible for training/logistics skills development, such as the former Skills for Logistics in the United Kingdom and the International Labour Organization (ILO)
4. Senior logistics and HR managers at multi-national logistics service providers (3PL) with extensive global recruitment
5. Representatives of organizations engaged in humanitarian and health logistics, such as the Humanitarian Logistics Association (HLA) and People that Deliver (PtD)

A comprehensive framework for the interviews was developed. The semi-structured setup gave the flexibility to gain new insights and take full advantage of the interviewees' expertise, while maintaining consistency across the sample.

Map 2.1 Countries Covered by Interviews

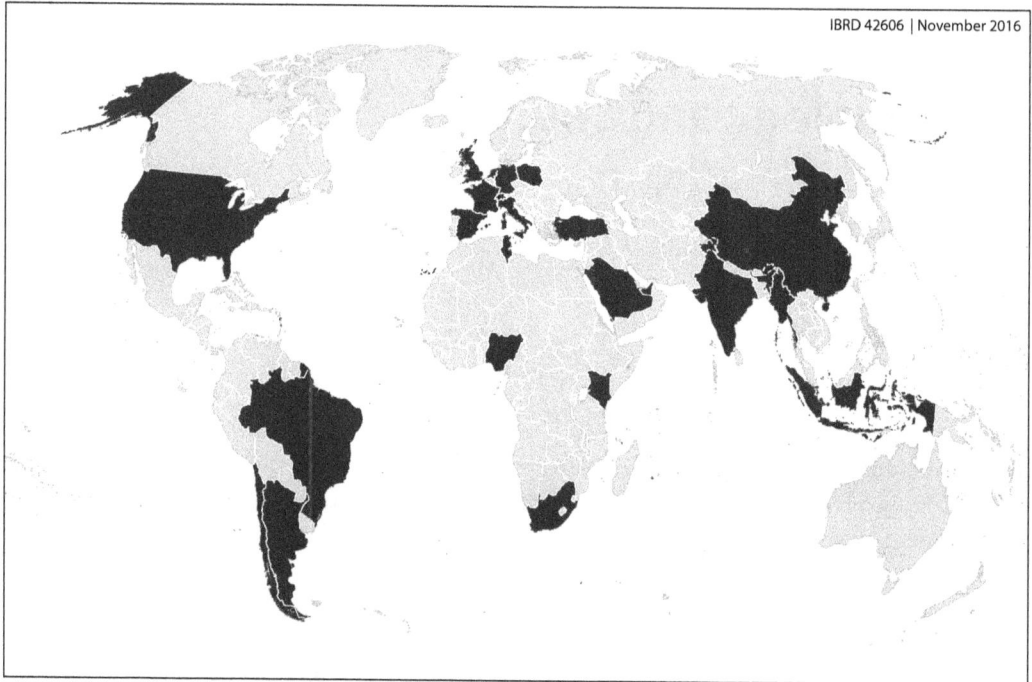

Table 2.1 **Interview Sample Overview**

Region	n	Sample job titles/descriptions
Europe	10	CEO of a logistics market intelligence agency Global VP of HR of a multi-national 3PL Professor of Logistics
South-East Asia	7	Former Country CEO of a multi-national 3PL Professor of SCM & Logistics Head of sales at a multi-national 3PL
The Americas	7	People development manager of a multi-national 3PL Human resource director LATAM at a multinational 3PL Economic Affairs Officer for South America
Sub-Saharan Africa	5	Professor of logistics Chairman of a large national 3PL President of a logistics training agency
Central Asia	5	CEO of a logistics recruitment agency CEO of a large Indian 3PL Certified CILT Trainer
Middle East/North Africa	2	CEO of a logistics recruitment agency Logistics consultant for a large transportation firm
Global View	2	Managers of globally operating NGOs
Total	**38**	

Survey: An online questionnaire was used to survey opinions more widely across all stakeholder groups, particularly those of logistics providers and industry associations. Invitations were circulated to participate in the survey via multiple channels: the CILT UK and CILT International membership lists, the HLA LinkedIn and Twitter followers, the ELA network and their sister country organizations (e.g., BVL, AILOG, CEL and PTL), and personal networks of interviewees or KLU affiliates. In total, 219 complete responses were received from around the world.

Table 2.2 shows the composition of the survey sample. The majority of responses came from Sub-Saharan Africa (47.5 percent), Europe (26.9 percent) and South-East Asia (10.5 percent). Third-party-logistics (3PL)

Table 2.2 Descriptive Statistics of Survey Sample

	n	%		n	%
Region			*Function*		
Sub-Saharan Africa	105	47.9	Supply chain management	73	33.3
Europe	59	26.9	Logistics	72	32.9
South-East Asia	23	10.5	General management	32	14.6
Middle East/North Africa	17	7.8	Human resources/training & development	11	5.0
Central Asia	9	4.1	Procurement	10	4.6
Other	6	2.8	Other	21	9.6
Total	**219**	**100**			
			Company revenue (in US$)		
Top 10 countries			Below 10 m	8	2.9
Zimbabwe	15	6.8	10–250 m	39	14.3
Nigeria	12	5.5	>250 m–1 b	38	13.9
Ghana	11	5.0	>1–10 b	90	33.0
Pakistan	11	5.0	Above 10 b	98	35.9
Romania	11	5.0			
Zambia	10	4.6	*Business experience (in years)*		
Greece	9	4.1	Less than 2	13	5.9
Uganda	9	4.1	2–5	12	5.5
Ukraine	9	4.1	>5–10	61	27.9
India	8	3.7	>10–25	100	45.7
			More than 25	33	15.1
Industry					
3PL (Transportation + Warehousing)	71	32.4	*Hierarchical level*		
Logistics association	30	13.7	Board level	19	8.7
Consulting/IT service	29	13.2	Senior management	81	37.0
Academia	27	12.3	Middle management	83	37.9
Transportation only	22	10.0	Lower management	21	9.6
Manufacturing	19	8.7	Non-managerial role	10	4.6
Retail/wholesale	15	6.8	Other	5	2.3
Warehousing only	6	2.7			

Logistics Competencies, Skills, and Training • http://dx.doi.org/10.1596/978-1-4648-1140-1

providers—the main target industry of this study—represented the largest group by a wide margin (32.4 percent). Overall, respondents were very experienced SCM and logistics managers (61 percent of whom had over 10 years business experience, and 84 percent were from middle, senior and C-level management), indicating high reliability and validity of the data. Respondents were asked to answer questions on the following topics:

1. Competence and skills shortages
2. Training and skills development
3. Recruitment, retention, and other HRM-related challenges

The results are presented in tables and figures both in the main report and Appendices. Frequently, "developing" and "developed" or high income regions are distinguished. The sub-sample from developing regions is based on 149 responses from Sub-Saharan Africa (68 percent), South-East Asia (15 percent), Middle East/North Africa (11 percent), and a few responses from Central Asia and Latin America (6 percent). The developed regions sub-sample comprised 64 responses from Europe (92 percent), Australia (6 percent) and North America (2 percent).

Focus group discussion: A focus group discussion was organized during the CILT International Convention, which took place in Dubai towards the end of this research project. This discussion helped validate the results of the interview and questionnaire surveys. Additional insights were acquired during the discussion. Forty-two delegates from 20 different countries participated in the 90-minute session. The countries represented included Zimbabwe, Nigeria, Tanzania, South Africa, Oman, Pakistan, Sri Lanka, Malaysia, China, Australia, Ukraine and the United Kingdom.

Literature review: The report builds on a comprehensive review of the skills and training literature in logistics and SCM. 70 relevant academic papers, reports and studies, are referred to at relevant points throughout the report to complement its own empirical findings. For further reading, a table of selected literature related to logistics skills, competence, and training is attached to this report (appendix A).

CHAPTER 3

The Quest for Logistics Competence: Survey Evidence

This chapter presents the findings of the global survey carried out in the report; the methodology of which has been described above

Previous Findings on Logistics Skills

According to Barnes and Liao (2012) "competencies are considered to be composed of the knowledge, skills, and abilities that are associated with high performance on the job at an individual level." Knowledge can be defined as "organized sets of principles and facts." Abilities are "enduring attributes of individuals that influence performance," and skills can be described as "developed capacities that facilitate learning or the further acquisition of knowledge" according to the O*NET Online initiative of the US Department of Labor (O*NET Online 2015). Several studies have investigated the role of individual competence in the logistics and SCM context, and have identified and classified essential competencies. For instance, Gammelgaard and Larson (2001) conducted surveys and case studies to identify core skills. They distinguish between quantitative/technological skills, SCM core skills, and interpersonal/managerial skills.

Harvey and Richey (2001) studied skills in a global setting, and found that supply chain managers need to possess managerial and transformation-based skills to compete in a global marketplace. Richey et al. (2006) suggest a high verbal IQ, strong achievement-orientation and high adaptability as the core SCM competencies for managers. Murphy and Poist (1991) developed a frequently used framework that distinguishes between business, logistics, and managerial (BLM) skill categories and includes a large number of precise skills.

Many companies around the world are finding it increasingly difficult to recruit enough skilled labor. Numerous researchers concur that HRM issues, especially concerning skills and competencies, are of critical importance to logistics and SCM (Cottrill & Rice Jr. 2012; Ellinger & Ellinger 2014; Fisher et al. 2010, and more). Despite the general agreement on their importance, between 2001 and 2005 only 4.5 percent of the articles in the three leading logistics journals addressed HRM issues (Murphy & Poist 2006).[1] More recently, Hohenstein, Feisel, and Hartmann (2014) could find only 109 HRM-related articles in 12 SCM and logistics journals from 1998 to 2014—just 0.57 papers per journal per annum. According to their systematic literature review, 87 percent of these articles addressed the issue of logistics competencies.

The interviews confirmed earlier literature (Hoberg et al. 2014) that logistics employees must possess a cross-functional understanding of various business fields, strategic decision-making, communication, leadership and inter-cultural skills and well developed analytical and IT skills in order to manage the manifold tasks they face on a daily basis. Logistics employees on all levels need to acquire the ability to think and work on a process basis. They need to look beyond their own functional and occupational silos and understand how their jobs connect to the entire process. Logistics has long been described as a "boundary-spanning" activity. The people working in this sector must be aware of the implications of their actions for the wider supply chain.

Besides these over-arching competencies, some requirements are highly dependent on the job type and hierarchical level. Employee groups need, therefore, to be split into different categories to review competence requirements, skill and employee shortages separately. Many classifications of logistics jobs have been developed and are in use today. The UK logistics skills council, Skills for Logistics, differentiated 10 levels in its "professional development stairway for logistics" (see chapter 6). A mature logistics job market would have an adequate supply of staff on each of these levels. The Chartered Institute of Logistics and Transport (CILT) uses a comprehensive "Professional Sector Map" in which they distinguish between different logistics sub-domains and personnel qualification stages (CILT 2015b).

Four Levels of Logistics Employment

The report investigates logistics competencies and training on a global scale. It compares logistics competence, training and the availability of staff across countries that are at different logistics maturity levels and subject to varying economic conditions. For this reason, the report distinguishes only four different occupations supply chain management. This is widely a simplification, considering the variety of jobs in each category, identified in the national professional guidelines (above) especially in Europe, such as the former UK Skills for Logistics.[2] A broad classification ensures that survey respondents and interviewees from both developing and developed regions are able to recognize the distinctions despite huge differences in sector maturity and individual job descriptions.

1. **Operative logistics/blue-collar staff**
   This group includes all logistics employees who carry out basic operational tasks and do not have any staff responsibility. Classic examples are truck drivers, forklift drivers and warehouse pickers.

2. **Administrative logistics staff**
   This level includes traffic planners, expediters, warehouse clerks, customs clearance officers and customer service employees. Staff at this level perform information-processing tasks and have limited supervisory or managerial responsibilities.

3. **Logistics supervisors**
   Supervisors have frontline responsibility, controlling logistics operations on the ground rather than in the office. Examples are shift leaders in warehouses or team leaders in a traffic department.

4. **Logistics managers**
   This category includes managerial staff, with higher-level decision-making responsibility. The extent of these responsibilities can range from junior through middle management roles to board level responsibility for logistics and supply chain strategy.

Widely Perceived Logistics Skills Shortages

Participants in the online survey were asked to rate the availability of suitably qualified personnel in their country at each of the four occupational levels. They used a discrete 5-point Likert scale (1 = very low, 5 = very high). As shown in figure 3.1, around 35–39 percent of respondents considering the availability at the operative, administrative and supervisory levels to be low or very low.

Figure 3.1 Availability of Suitably Qualified Logistics Staff (All Regions)

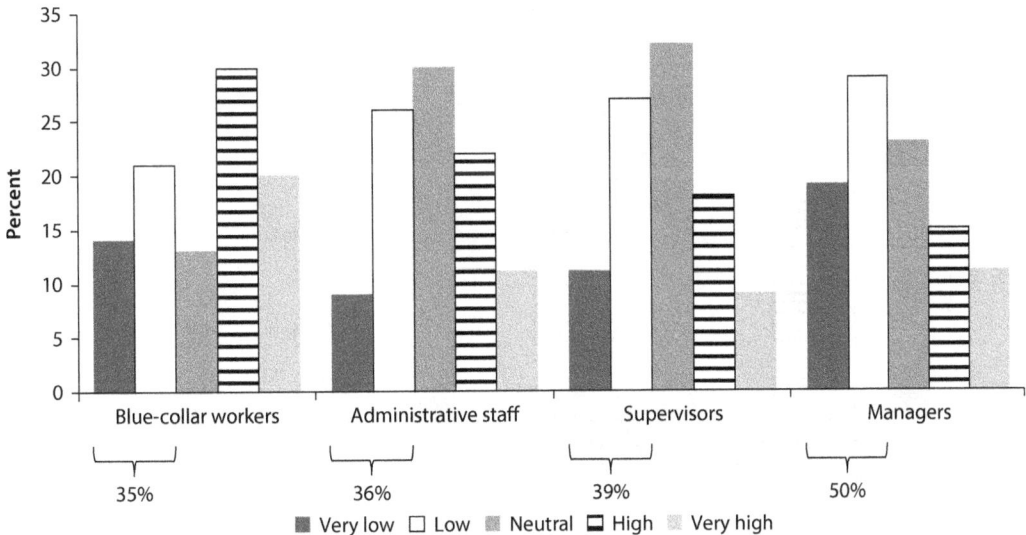

It was at the managerial level where the shortage was most acute with half the sample judging the availability of personnel with the right qualifications to be low or very low.

A geographical disaggregation of the survey results reveals a marked difference between developing and developed regions (figure 3.2). In the former, the main shortage of suitable personnel is at the managerial level, with over half the

Figure 3.2 Availability of Suitably Qualified Logistics Staff in Emerging (Developing) and Developed Regions

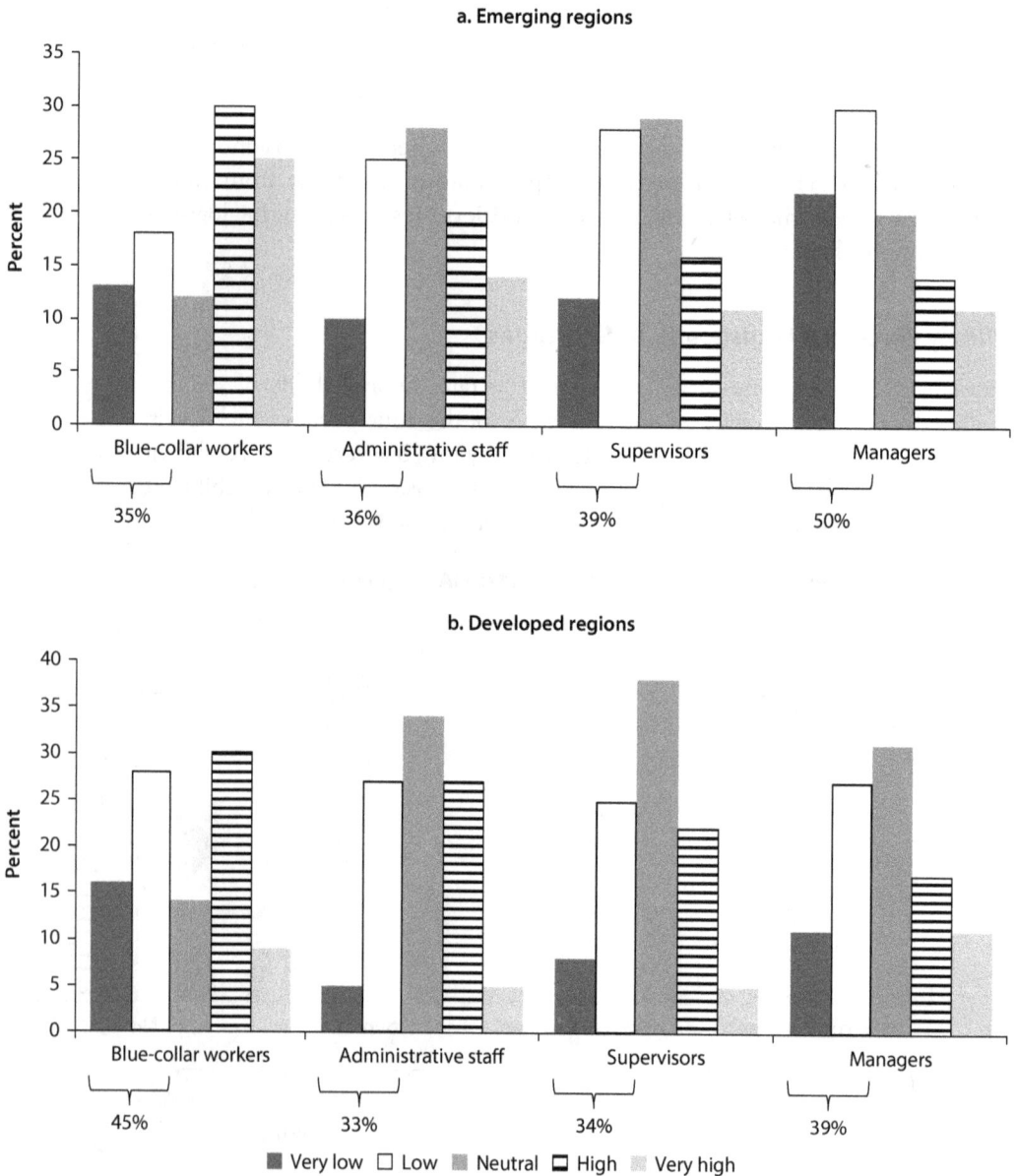

a. Emerging regions

b. Developed regions

Very low ☐ Low ☐ Neutral ☐ High ☐ Very high

respondents rating availability as low or very low, while in developed countries the results are skewed in the opposite direction, indicating that the main problem is finding enough staff at the operational level. The availability of supervisory staff is also significantly lower in developing markets.

The survey also shed light on the importance and availability of particular competencies at each of the four occupational levels. These competencies were divided into six categories and rated using the same 5-point scale (figure 3.3).

The four graphs show that virtually all competence categories are deemed to be of high importance (average around 4/5). Employees on all levels need to perform these tasks effectively, be communicative, possess technical and personal skills and be able to learn and acquire further knowledge on a regular basis. Supervisors and managers complement the basic skill sets with leadership skills. The high importance attached to all the competence categories confirms the results of previous research, which showed that logisticians must possess very diverse skills sets to master all the challenges they routinely face.

A comparison of the importance and availability scores suggests that there is a serious skills shortage in all groups and across all competence categories. While respondents assign a high importance (an average of approximately 4) to almost all competence categories, they rated availability considerably lower (typically 2.8–2.9). It is perhaps surprising that there is little variability around these average scores. It reflects a general view that all six competencies are equally important and in similarly short supply.

Figure 3.3 Importance and Availability Rating of Logistics Competencies at Occupational Levels

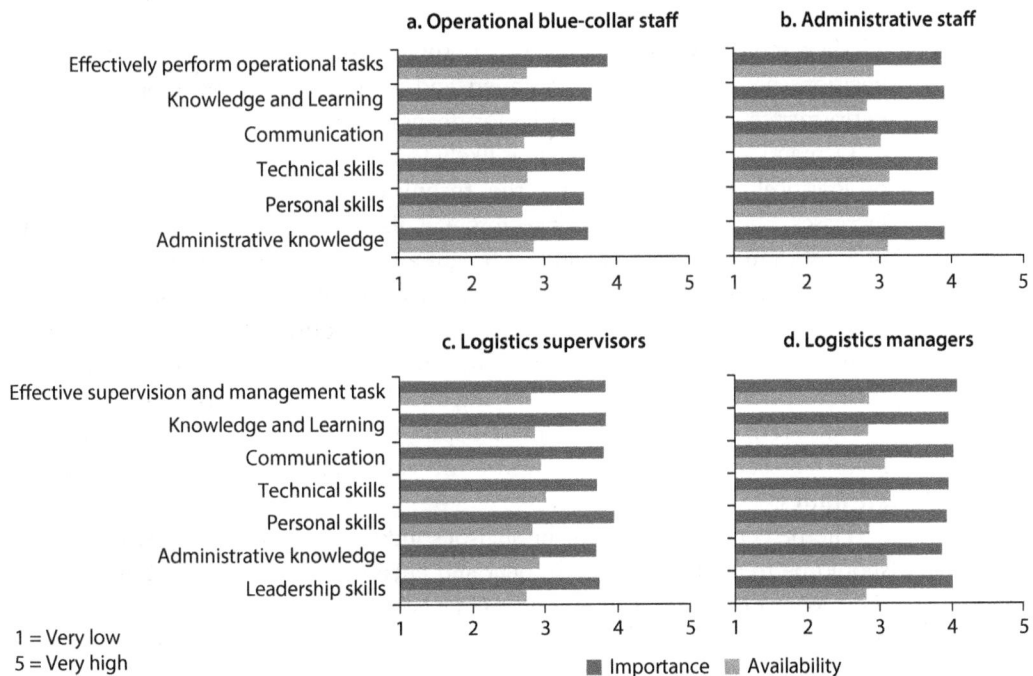

1 = Very low
5 = Very high

■ Importance ■ Availability

Interviewees shed further light on this skill availability issue. They argued that the problem is two-fold. On the one hand, positions are often simply vacant because insufficient staff are available in the job market with the right skills and qualifications. The skills shortage has another important dimension. This is the skill deficiency across the existing logistics workforce, much of which has not kept up-to-date with technical innovations, operating procedures and changing market dynamics. Several specific skills shortages were frequently highlighted by the interviewees.

Logistics blue-collar workers often lack the attitude or discipline to perform well in their job. In particular, older workers may have limited enthusiasm for training partly because they believe that their extensive experience renders it unnecessary or because they are nearing the end of their careers. Sometimes they are also afraid and skeptical of new technologies, while younger workers more easily adapt to new IT. Furthermore, blue-collar and administrative staff can have limited awareness of their role in the supply chain and cannot ascertain the impact of their actions. This "silo thinking" often leads to glitches that could be avoided if more logistics employees had a better appreciation of their role within the wider supply system.

As indicated by the survey results, leadership and communication skills are essential for supervisors and managers. Unfortunately, these are the skills they most often lack. Leaders can climb the career ladder due mainly to their technical skills and knowledge. Often they are put in charge of a whole department without having had any previous exposure to leadership roles or leadership-related training. They often struggle to make strategic decisions or perform long-term planning, since these qualifications were not required in their previous positions.

Many interviewees noted that supervisors are often unable to make data-driven decisions because they do not understand what the cost drivers are or which performance indicators are crucial for financial success.

Demand for skilled logisticians is likely to continue to grow rapidly as the level of logistical activity rises and the technical sophistication of the function increases. The growth of other sectors will also depend indirectly on the ability of logistics to cope with expanding freight and trade volumes. Logistics will only be able to do this if it is adequately staffed with skilled employees.

Most logistics-related activity is now outsourced to the 3PL sector. The large 3PL companies with multi-national coverage need to "customize" their workforce to the logistical characteristics of the countries in which they operate, reflecting the freight modal split, the industry and product mix, the level of technology, the structure of the logistics market and cultural attributes.

The perception of jobs in the logistics industry needs to change. Employees should be treated with more respect and encouraged to feel proud of the work they do. As discussed in greater detail in a later section, more positive images can be presented of logistics work, showing the vital role it plays in the functioning of an economy and society.

Shortage of qualified personnel on all levels facilitates a "war for talent"—not only between competing companies in the logistics sector but also across industries. Since many workers in logistics jobs are paid low wages compared to other industries, for example, manufacturing or health care, it is hardly surprising that logistics companies struggle to find enough recruits during periods of high employment.

A recruitment shortfall has several consequences. Firstly, if positions stay vacant for a period of time, colleagues need to work extra hours to compensate. That usually leads to a loss in service quality. Secondly, high labor turnover and/or an over-reliance on a temporary agency staff can adversely affect productivity and quality. The new employees' need to adjust to the tasks and working environment and to seek assistance from colleagues often drags down the output of entire departments.

Thirdly, a company is less likely to invest in training employees if there is a high probability of them leaving. An interviewee asked "Why should I train my employees and make them ready to join a competitor?" Another stated that "logistics training can be like putting water in a leaking sieve. A whole market approach was needed to deal with the problem of skills shortages." This mindset is a serious threat to the logistics community and was highlighted as a dilemma that logistics managers frequently face when they make decisions on training and training-related budgets.

A recent multi-national survey by Cap Gemini et al. (2016, p. 37) of the users and providers of logistics services has confirmed that there is a serious and worsening skills shortage in the logistics sector. Just over half of the shippers using these services felt that they could rely on their service providers "to address the labor shortage's effect on their business". Their confidence may be misplaced, however, as 79 percent of the service providers consulted felt that "they are unprepared for the labor shortage's impact on their supply chain". The same survey also enquired about the impact of the logistics labor/skills shortage on the businesses affected. Respectively 61 percent, 52 percent, and 48 percent of the respondents considered it to be adversely affecting product or service quality, impairing productivity and causing wage inflation. Around third of the companies consulted felt it was causing them to "settle into a low-skill equilibrium" or to change their business model.

Respondents to the online survey were also asked what they considered to be the main HR challenges likely to face the logistics sector over the next five years (figure 3.4). There was general agreement between those in developed and developing regions about the relative importance of these challenges, though some notable differences emerged. Challenges deemed to be "major" received significantly higher percentages from respondents in developing markets, suggesting that overall they will face greater difficult in recruiting, retaining and training logistics staff than their counterparts in developed countries. Across both regions, however, recruiting at the managerial level, keeping logistics salaries competitive and succession planning were at or near the top of the list of future HR challenges. Responses from the developed world prioritized the need to develop leadership skills. At the other end of the spectrum, recruiting operational

Figure 3.4 Future HRM Challenges in Logistics in Developed and Emerging (Developing) Regions

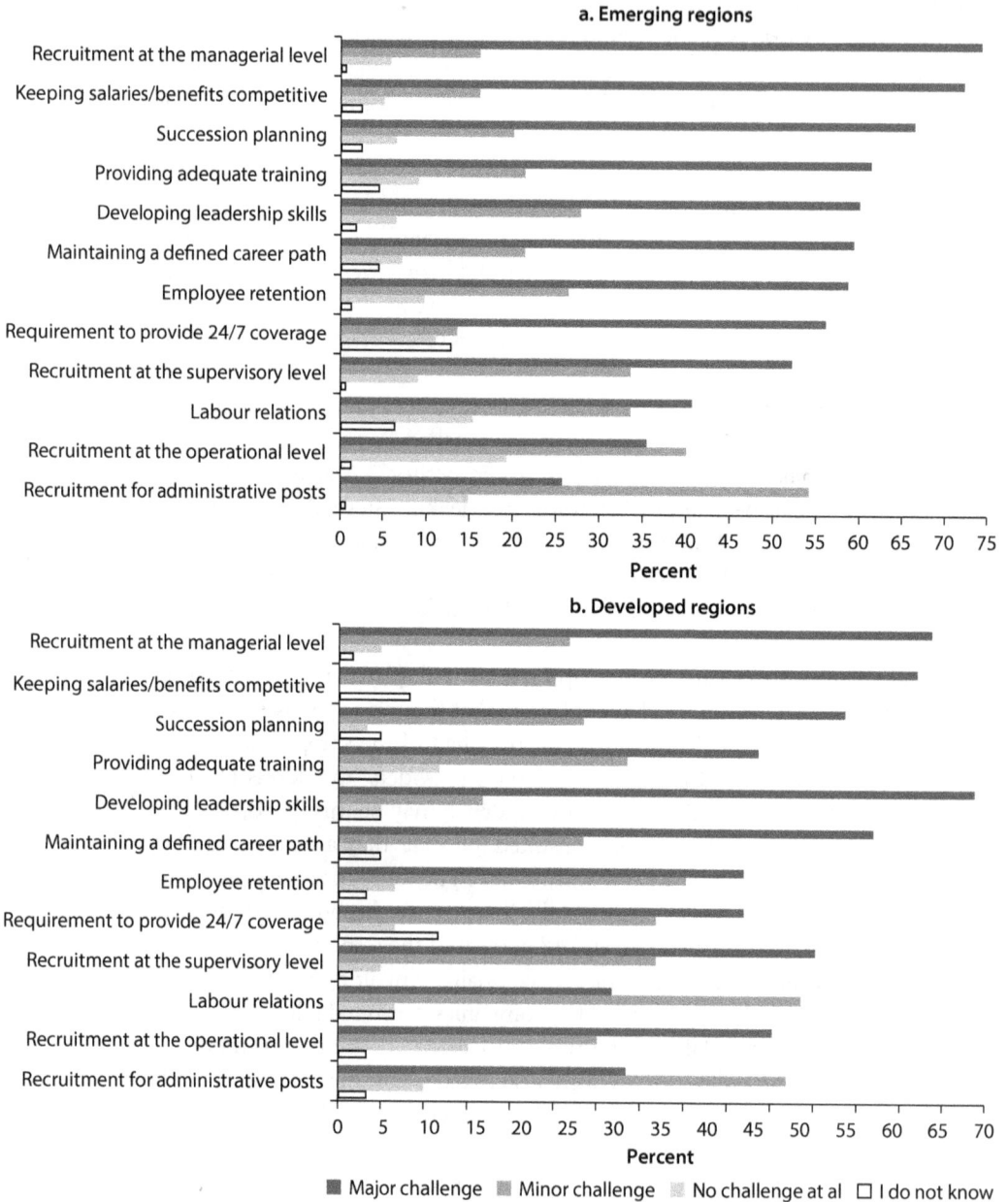

a. Emerging regions

b. Developed regions

Major challenge   Minor challenge   No challenge at al   ☐ I do not know

and administrative personnel were regarded as predominantly "minor challenges" by contributors from developing markets. Almost half of those in developed countries, however, felt that recruiting staff for operational roles in logistics would be a major challenge.

A lack of senior executives with the necessary capabilities to manage complex global supply chains could have a negative effect on the growth of international trade. In recent years there have been numerous initiatives to promote trade facilitation by "expediting the movement, release and clearance of goods" mainly through the streamlining of customs and other administrative procedures at international borders. Trade can also be facilitated by ensuring that businesses engaging in international trade have enough managers equipped with the skills needed to design, implement and control international logistics systems. This aspect of trade facilitation is seldom mentioned, but one which will merit greater attention if, as our survey suggests, companies experience increasing difficulty in finding the next generation of top-level supply chain managers.

Its adverse effect on international trade and economic development is only one of several externalities arising from the logistics skills gap. There is also likely to be an environmental externality, as under-trained operators of freight vehicles drive less fuel-efficiently and hence are responsible for higher levels of exhaust emissions per kilometer travelled. In addition, they drive less safely and have a higher level of involvement in traffic accidents. Accident rates in warehouses and freight terminals are also higher where staff are not properly trained. The resulting social and health costs represent a further set of externalities.

Reasons for Shortages

There are numerous reasons for the skills shortages observed at all employee levels, across different regions and between countries within the same region. The interviews and online survey results highlighted shortages at the blue-collar level, even in emerging economies with large, young populations. Operative logistics positions, such as those of long-haul truck drivers, warehouse pickers and forklift drivers, appear unappealing and are linked to low social status and poor wages. The nature of these tasks often involve long working hours, night shifts and, in the case of truck drivers, long periods away from home. These conditions make it difficult to recruit people and fill vacant positions. Many low-level operational logistics jobs are uninteresting to large sections of the population, for example, in India (truck driving regarded as low skill job) or Thailand (logistics jobs filled by migrants from the Lao People's Democratic Republic or Myanmar).

In many countries—both developing and developed—logistics activity has become clustered in major hubs. As Sheffi (2013) discusses in detail, there are major agglomeration benefits in concentrating logistical facilities in strategic locations. One of the shortcomings of clustering is that it intensifies the competition for logistics labor in small areas. Recruitment becomes even more difficult where the logistics hub is located away from major population centers. For instance, Magna Park near Lutterworth is one of the largest warehouse and logistics parks in the United Kingdom. It is centrally located but has a limited employment pool in the immediate vicinity.

Locations are often attractive because they are central, have lower prices and sometimes offer favorable tax regimes, but they are less than ideal from an HR standpoint. While lower costs are an upside of remote locations, a limited supply of labor is certainly a major downside. Firms struggle to find enough people, let alone qualified ones. In low income countries where levels of personal mobility are low, recruitment is typically confined to smaller catchment areas than in developed countries. There can also be HR issues particular to certain localities. An interviewee from Russia highlighted the problem of alcoholism in remote areas that leads to high levels of absenteeism, low productivity levels and, ultimately, safety issues. Worker satisfaction also tends to be lower in remote areas, since many employees are forced to commute long distances from home to work.

This labor availability problem also exists at the urban scale, where the decentralization of warehousing from inner-urban zones to sub-urban and out-of-town locations has significantly increased journey-to-work distances. Given high levels of traffic congestion, particularly in mega-cities in emerging economies, and the high commuting costs relative to the modest wage rates prevalent in the logistics sector, this geographical shift in warehousing capacity is reckoned to have exacerbated the shortage on logistics labor.

In wealthier countries the pursuit of white-collar office jobs, offering higher social status, more convenient and comfortable office work and better career opportunities, leaves many operational positions vacant. The problem appears to be less acute in Germany, where a structured dual-education/apprenticeship scheme has been in place for decades to provide technical and operative workforces. The collaboration between vocational schools and logistics companies creates a theoretically- and practically-educated workforce for a range of (at least initially) non-managerial positions. Due to the high level of education in the vocational schools, a career in technical and operational roles is well respected socially.

Changes in the nature of order-picking operations have made warehouse employment less appealing in several sectors. Jobs have become more routine, more tightly controlled and monitored, more monotonous and often more stressful. The growth of online retailing has created a huge new demand for labor in item-level picking, often in huge, impersonal fulfillment centers. The working conditions, salaries and career prospects there often fall short of the expectations of potential recruits. In more traditional warehouses, advances in IT and materials handling have often resulted in deskilling and demotivation of the workforce. On the other hand, by making the work less manually-demanding, new technology can extend the range of possible recruits by age and gender. By improving productivity it can also reduce the total demand for labor.

There is a cultural dimension to companies' difficulties in finding enough logistics employees with the right skills and aptitudes. Cultural norms rather than a lack of competencies can impair their ability to perform logistics jobs adequately. Hofstede investigated this topic. His well-known cultural dimensions theory explains cross-cultural communication in terms of six underlying dimensions: power-distance, individualism, uncertainty avoidance, masculinity, long-term orientation, and indulgence (Hofstede 1980). As mentioned earlier, global logistics businesses employ a large number of people with diverse cultural backgrounds and must be aware of cross-cultural differences and characteristics. The following country example from a senior logistics manager working for a multi-national 3PL in Indonesia illustrates the role of culture in managing a multicultural workforce.

Hofstede's power-distance index measures the extent to which less powerful members of organizations and institutions accept their situation and expect power to be distributed unequally. He also distinguishes between individualism and collectivism, the latter being the degree to which individuals are integrated into groups. Some societies are strongly collectivist, where people are integrated into strong, cohesive in-groups at birth and can count on their protection in exchange for unquestioning loyalty (Hofstede 1980). Indonesia ranks high on the power-distance index, low on the individualism index and is essentially collectivist. Indonesian employees typically perceive their superiors as being powerful, distant and of high social status. On the other hand, peers and colleagues are almost as close as family members. They thrive in an atmosphere of harmony.

This cultural trait can lead to problems at the logistics workplace, as highlighted by the expert interviewee. His subordinates are "afraid" of him and very reluctant to report disruptions or admit mistakes, even if doing so would minimize the chances of problems escalating. Even worse, they do not inform colleagues on the same hierarchical level of mistakes, since they do not want to hurt "family members." Even Indonesian logistics professionals with strong educational backgrounds and extensive logistics experience and knowledge can under-perform for these cultural reasons. Overall, it took the interviewee a year to achieve a shift in the mindset of his locally recruited team. By highlighting the importance of constructive criticism and regularly providing feedback, he was able to foster open and honest horizontal and vertical communication. This goes beyond traditional competence-based training, presenting an important HR challenge for logistics companies operating in different cultural settings.

Notes

1. Journal of Business Logistics, International Journal of Physical Distribution & Logistics Management, Transportation Journal.

2. Skills for Logistics, the former UK sector skills council for logistics, was closed in January 2015.

References

Barnes, J., and Y. Liao. 2012. "The Effect of Individual, Network, and Collaborative Competencies on the Supply Chain Management System." *International Journal of Production Economics* 140 (2): 888–99.

Cap Gemini, PennState Smeal College of Business, Penske, and Korn Ferry. 2016. "Third-Party Logistics Study: The State of Logistics Outsourcing." www.3plstudy.com.

CILT. 2015b. *Professional Development Directory 2015—Training and Qualifications*. The Chartered Institute of Logistics and Transport. http://www.aspire-cilt.org.uk/wp -content/uploads/Training-Directory-2015.pdf.

Cottrill, K., and J. B. Rice Jr. 2012. "Supply Chain Talent Management: Adressing the HR Disconnect." *MIT Center for Transportation & Logistics White Paper* (Winter): 1–16.

Ellinger, A. E., and A. D. Ellinger. 2014. "Leveraging Human Resource Development Expertise to Improve Supply Chain Managers' Skills and Competencies." *European Journal of Training and Development* 38 (1/2): 118–35.

Fisher, S. L., M. E. Graham, S. Vachon, and A. Vereecke. 2010. "Guest Editors' Note: Don't Miss the Boat: Research on HRM and Supply Chains." *Human Resource Management* 49 (5): 813–28.

Gammelgaard, B., and P. D. Larson. 2001. "Logistics Skills and Competencies for Supply Chain Management." *Journal of Business Logistics* 22 (2): 27–50.

Harvey, M. G., and R. G. Richey. 2001. "Global Supply Chain Management: The Selection of Globally Competent Managers." *Journal of International Management* 7: 105–28.

Hoberg, K., K. Alicke, C. Flöthmann, and J. Lundin. 2014. "The DNA of Supply Chain Executives." *Supply Chain Management Review* (November): 36–43.

Hofstede, G. 1980. *Culture's Consequences: International Differences in Work-Related Values*. Sage Publications, Inc.

Hohenstein, N.-O., E. Feisel, and E. Hartmann. 2014. "Human Resource Management Issues in Supply Chain Management Research: A Systematic Literature Review from 1998 to 2014." *International Journal of Physical Distribution & Logistics Management* 44 (6): 434–63.

Murphy, P., and R. Poist. 1991. "Skill Requirements of Senior-Level Logistics Executives: An Empirical Investigation." *Journal of Business Logistics* 12 (2): 73–95.

———. 2006. "Skill Requirements of Contemporary Senior-and Entry-Level Logistics Managers: A Comparative Analysis." *Transportation Journal* 45 (3): 46–60.

O*NET Online. 2015. *Definition of Knowledge, Skills, and Abilities*. (accessed August 10, 2015), https://www.onetonline.org/.

Richey, R. G., R. Tokman, & A. R. Wheeler. 2006. "A Supply Chain Manager Selection Methodology: Empirical Test and Suggested Application." *Journal of Business Logistics* 27 (2): 163–90.

Sheffi, Y. 2013. "Logistics-Intensive Clusters: Global Competitiveness and Regional Growth." In *Handbook of Global Logistics*, 463–500. New York: Springer Science+Business Media.

CHAPTER 4

Sector Case Studies

This chapter comprises two case studies which illustrate in greater detail the nature of the logistics skills shortage in sectors that have attracted a high deal of attention in recent years: trucking and humanitarian logistics. The shortage of truck drivers is currently the highest profile logistics skills issue in terms of company concerns, political lobbying and media coverage. Although it has not gained as much publicity, the lack of logistics expertise in organizations providing emergency relief and humanitarian support, mainly in low income countries, is believed to be constraining the efficiency and effectiveness of their operations.

Truck Drivers

The driver shortage problem mainly afflicts the more developed countries, though is also acute in several emerging markets, such as India (Dash 2011), South Africa (Anon 2014a) and Brazil (2014b). It is not a new problem. As Sheffi (2015) has recently acknowledged "a shortage of truck drivers has bedeviled the logistics industry for so long that it's difficult to image a time when filling driver vacancies was not a problem." For example, back in 1998 the American Trucking Association Foundation commissioned a study of the truck driver shortage problem. A subsequent study by Global Insights (2005) for the American Trucking Associations in 2005 projected that the shortage of "heavy duty truck drivers" in the US would swell from 22,000 in 2004 to 111,000 by 2014. This latter figure proved an overestimate as the shortage is currently around 35,000–40,000 (Sheffi 2015). In absolute terms, however, this is still a very large number and one which is creating difficulties for many US businesses. Some commentators have suggested that the US driver shortage is having a macro-economic impact through the inflationary pressures exerted by rising labor costs in the road freight sector.

The "shortage of qualified personnel in road freight transport" in the EU in 2008 was deemed serious enough to justify an inquiry by the Transport and Tourism Committee of the European Parliament. This concluded that the EU needed an additional 74,480 truck drivers that year. Expressed as a percentage of the total trucking driving workforce, the shortage was greatest in the Czech Republic, the Netherlands, Spain and Portugal. One survey in 2012 suggested that 84 percent of European road haulage companies were having difficulty recruiting drivers (Rauwald and Schmidt 2012). Currently, it appears that Germany and the United Kingdom have the most serious problems among the EU member states. It is estimated that over the next 10–15 years around 40 percent of German truck drivers will retire, which will create a shortfall of 150,000 drivers (Weiss 2013). In the United Kingdom, the Road Haulage Association and Freight Transport Association assess the "national driver shortage" to be around 45,000 and 52,000 respectively, with another 35,000 drivers likely to retire in the next two years who will be extremely difficult to replace. The expectation in Europe, as in North America, is that the driver shortage will escalate over the next 5–10 years.

There is also evidence of the problem seriously affecting the trucking industries of emerging markets. The Transport Corporation of India (TCI 2015), the country's largest logistics provider, has declared that "while the West is already facing an acute shortage of truck drivers, Indian industry, which was comfortably placed, suddenly finds itself staring at a problem which could have been avoided with greater resourcefulness and to which, regrettably, there are no easy and quick fix solutions." It has been suggested that around 10 percent of the Indian truck fleet is unused because of a lack of drivers, "in a country with high unemployment and a bountiful supply of labor."

Reports suggest that there is shortfall of around 100,000 qualified drivers in Brazil and that Brazilian carriers are having to recruit drivers from Colombia (Anon 2014b). It is estimated that South Africa needs an extra 15,000 truck drivers each year but in recent years the supply has fallen well short of this target (Magutu 2015).

In recognition of the serious and widespread occurrence of the truck driver shortage, the International Road Transport Union (IRU) adopted in 2010 a "resolution on driver shortages and strategies for better recruitment and retention" which provided advice to governments, national road transport associations and companies on how to deal with the problem. It was based on the premise that "increased transport demand" will be "increasingly constrained and disrupted by driver shortages across the world's economies."

In countries where the enforcement of employment and transport regulations is often lax and open to corruption, a lack of qualified drivers can result in trucks being driven by untrained and unlicensed personnel to the detriment of operational productivity, road safety and the environment. This can undermine efforts to upgrade the professional status of logistics in these countries.

Reasons for the Driver Shortage

The shortage is the result of numerous, inter-related factors and this is partly why it is proving so difficult to correct. Some of these factors are generic, others specific to individual countries. The main factors are as follows:

Growth in the demand for road freight transport: Road is by far the dominant freight transport mode and in many countries the growth in road ton-kms is closely coupled to economic growth. Although labor productivity in road haulage has been increasing, it has been outpaced by the growth in freight traffic.

Relative unattractiveness of the occupation: Various aspects of truck driving make it unappealing to potential recruits:

Low wage rates: In a sense, the truck driver shortage is evidence of a market failure. In a free market economy, wage rates should be bid up to a level at which enough workers enter the profession. As Sheffi (2015) argues, "shippers, while complaining about driver shortages, are still not willing to pay more for high quality truck transportation. In other words, the situation is not 'bad enough', despite the publicity." As a result most carriers lack the resources to substantially increase the level of driver remuneration, which typically represents 30–40 percent of total operating costs. Some of the larger US carriers are now paying "signing bonuses" of between $500 and $12,000, mainly to poach drivers from other carriers (Cary 2014). For the majority of smaller trucking businesses that cannot afford such bonuses, this merely exacerbates the problem. Very low rates of pay, coupled with the need to pay bribes, have been highlighted as a major cause of the Indian driver shortage (TCI 2015).

Working conditions: Truck drivers often have to put up with unsocial hours, poor amenities, stress and, according to Kemp et al. (2013), "emotional exhaustion." These conditions have deteriorated with the move to 24/7 delivery, tightening just-in-time schedules and more rigid timing of inbound deliveries. The driver shortage is most acute in the long haul sector of the road freight market where time spent away from home is greatest. This has been one of the fastest growing sectors of the market as centralisation and wider sourcing have been extending supply lines. In the meantime, the life-style expectations of employees have been rising. With adequate financial compensation more workers would accept the adversities of a truck driver's life, but not at the prevailing wage levels. The working conditions of European or American truck drivers, although much criticized, are still far superior to those of their counterparts in low and middle income economies. In India, for example, drivers can be away from home for weeks at a time, spend many hours waiting at check points, often drive on very poor roads in badly maintained, uncomfortable vehicles with no access to roadside amenities, and can be forced to work excessive hours to earn a basic income.

Changing nature of the job: It has been argued that truck driving now offers less job satisfaction because driving performance is constantly monitored by onboard devices and the work much more "codified" and structured than before (European Parliament 2009). It has been argued that "the romance of the role of truck driver—the lone hero, his rig, the adventure of the wide, open road—has vanished, if it ever existed" (Anon 2015). One can advance a counter argument, however, that technology has made the job easier and safer. The need to master all the technology on a modern truck has also led to some "upskilling" and diversification of the average driver's skill set.

Image: The public image of the trucking industry is often poor and the social status of drivers considered low.

Increased regulation: The Working Time Directive (WTD) in the EU and tightening controls on drivers hours in many countries have increased the number of drivers required to perform a given road freight task, particularly in the long-haul sector. On the other hand, these regulations, which have been motivated mainly by safety concerns, have helped improve working conditions for drivers. According to the 2009 European Parliament study the net effect of these regulations has been neutral. Yet it has been suggested that the United States have aggravated the driver shortage problem (Morris 2015).

Demographics: The age structure of the truck driver population in the US and Europe is a major cause for concern. The average age of a US truck driver is 47 (Soergel 2015). In the United Kingdom it is 53, with 62 percent of drivers over 45 and only 2 percent under 25. The sector has not been attracting sufficient young people into the profession to replace the older generations soon to retire. As discussed above, this is partly due to truck driving becoming less appealing relative to other competing occupations and not being seen as a "career of choice." Other factors have also constrained the influx of younger recruits. In the United Kingdom and United States, for example, high insurance costs make it expensive for carriers to employ drivers under 25 and this insurance penalty has been increasing. The ending of compulsory military service in several European countries is also reckoned to have had a detrimental effect on recruitment as many young people formerly qualified as truck drivers during their period of conscription.

Qualification requirements: It has been claimed that some potential recruits are being deterred by the higher levels of qualification and certification now required to become a truck driver and the higher cost of obtaining them, which in many cases has to be borne by the applicant. In the EU, for example, it has become mandatory for drivers to have a "certificate of professional competence" (CPC) in addition to their heavy goods vehicle (HGV) driving licence. In the US, more thorough checks on the past conduct of applicants tend to exclude people who in the past would have been employed in the trucking industry. In South Africa, only around 5–10 percent of applicants for truck driving jobs are "deemed suitable for training" (Anon 2014a). If it is true that increased certification and tougher checks are inhibiting recruitment, they may be temporarily exacerbating the problem, but in the longer term they should upgrade professional standards and address the image/status problem mentioned earlier. The dampening effect on recruitment may also be exaggerated. Obtaining a driver CPC, for example, requires only 35 hours of training over five years.

Industry structure: In all countries the trucking industry is highly fragmented. Typically around 80 percent of carriers have fewer than five vehicles and around 40–50 percent of businesses have a single vehicle run by an "owner-driver." This high proportion of sole-employee businesses means that the driver needs to have entrepreneurial skills as well as competence as a driver. They must see the trucking industry as an attractive commercial prospect as well as a source of employment. The driver shortage is generally portrayed in the media as trucking companies failing to recruit enough "employee drivers," but this overlooks the fact that much of a country's freight is moved in trucks owned by the driver as a sole trader.

In recent years, many owner drivers have been leaving the business because of low margins, poor returns and retirement. Those retiring have found it increasingly difficult to pass on the business to the next generation because, for the reasons listed above, trucking is perceived as a down-market activity. Inadequate business formation and survival rates at the owner-driver end of the trucking industry is another aspect of the market failure outlined earlier. In some countries, owner-drivers get some or all of their capital from family members, who must also be convinced that trucking represents a good medium- to long-term investment. Entry barriers to the road freight sector are not solely financial. In regulated trucking markets it can be difficult for owner-drivers to obtain licenses, while in some countries new entrants are deterred by the efforts of incumbents to maintain a "closed shop" for road haulage services often by illegal means.

Solutions to the Problem

It is generally accepted that there is no single solution to the driver shortage problem. Several initiatives could help to ease the current problem and keep the future shortfall of drivers within manageable limits:

Increase wage levels: This is the market solution. If shippers are unable to move their freight by road or to use an alternative transport mode, freight rates will have to rise to incentivize more people to come into the industry and drive the trucks. In most countries, carriers' margins are so thin that they have little slack to pay drivers more and so most of the financial burden will fall on shippers. The fact that the driver shortage problem persists even in countries such as the US and Switzerland where drivers are relatively well paid suggests that improving remuneration is unlikely to be enough.

Improve working conditions: Some companies have shown how it is possible to change shift patterns and delivery schedules to minimize unsocial hours (Kilcarr 2015). This often adds cost, but can still be a cheaper option than employing "agency drivers" at short notice or risk losing business. In Brazil, the National Confederation of Transport (CNT) has established a network of centers around the country at which truck drivers can access a range of welfare, medical and recreational services while they are away from home. This is significantly improving working conditions in the Brazilian trucking industry.

Logistics Competencies, Skills, and Training • http://dx.doi.org/10.1596/978-1-4648-1140-1

Improving the image of truck driving: As the European Parliament report explains this can be done by "by promoting campaigns on the key role played by the transport sector in the economy, as well as providing information on employment prospects to schools, employment services and the media." Such campaigns can be run by trade bodies, professional associations, government agencies and larger logistics providers. This should not simply be seen in presentational and perceptual terms. The overall professional status of truck driving needs to be enhanced, through better training, apprenticeships and improved career development.

Changing nature of the job: Although sometimes presented as a negative factor, particularly in encouraging the premature departure of older drivers, there are many positive developments that should be attractive to younger recruits. These include the increased technological sophistication of trucks, greater application of IT, sleeker vehicle designs and the closer integration of truck driving into the logistics management process.

Increasing the participation of women and ethnic minorities: In Europe and North America truck driving is predominantly a job for white males. It is estimated that only around 6 percent of US truck drivers are female (Hsu 2016). It is a sector than needs to have a more open and inclusive recruitment policy and to do more to attract women and members of ethnic minorities.

Immigration: Truck driver shortages in the past have been partly relieved by migration. For example following the enlargement of the EU in 2003 many Eastern European drivers migrated to the United Kingdom to fill haulage industry vacancies. Among the recent influx of migrants to the EU may be aspiring truck drivers. The International Road Transport Union (IRU) is trying to achieve greater international harmonization and recognition of truck driver qualifications to increase the mobility of employees in this sector. There is a danger, however, that countries will poach each other's drivers, shifting the problem and not fundamentally correcting it.

Government intervention: Given the current scarcity of truck drivers and potentially damaging effect on national economic performance, it may be necessary for governments to intervene. In the United Kingdom, for example, the government has decided to "review the speed with which heavy goods vehicle (HGV) driving tests and driver medical assessments currently take place and will consider options to accelerate both in order to help address the shortage of qualified HGV drivers" (Cassidy 2015). The UK Road Haulage Association wants it to go further and provide grants of up to £3,000 to prospective drivers to cover the cost of their training. Government can also play a useful role in upgrading road-side facilities for truck drivers. In low and middle income countries, governments can help to make driving a truck more palatable by reducing related bureaucratic checks, curbing corruption, providing more medical support etc, though all this involves tackling systemic problems within the country.

Improvements in productivity: It is possible to decouple labor requirements from the growth of road freight volumes by increasing productivity. This is particularly important in developing countries where labor productivity in the road freight sector is relatively low. Productivity can be improved in various ways:

Increasing the maximum size and weight of trucks: This permits the consolidation of freight in fewer vehicles. High capacity vehicles are widely used in Australia, New Zealand, Sweden, Finland, the Netherlands, South Africa and some US states, though their legalization is a highly controversial issue at the EU level in Europe and the federal level in the US.

Promoting horizontal collaboration in supply chains: This involves companies sharing vehicle capacity to maximize load factors.

Improved load matching: Greater use of online freight exchanges and procurement platforms helps companies find backloads and can eliminate many empty return journeys.

Platooning and automation: These innovations have been suggested as offering a technical fix to the driver shortage problem. The use of so-called "electronic tow-bars" to link a convoy of trucks would allow the "platoon" to be driven by a single driver. The other vehicles would have drivers in the cab, but, as they would not be driving, they could be on their rest breaks. The same situation would apply to automated trucks which could move independently. The US State of Nevada has recently approved trials of "self-driving" trucks on public roads (Thielman 2015). Both technologies would represent an injection of capital into the road freight sector to reduce its dependence on labor. They could ease the driver shortage problem, partly by circumventing drivers' hours restrictions, though they will have minimal, if any, impact on the problem in the short to medium term.

Humanitarian Logistics

The increasing frequency and intensity of both natural and man-made disasters, mainly in low and middle income countries, is creating a growing demand for specialists in so-called "humanitarian logistics." They generally work for the relief agencies, such as the World Food Program, Oxfam and Médecins sans Frontières, which must mobilize a broad range of resources at short notice to rescue populations afflicted by disasters. Van Wassenhove (2006) estimated that 80 percent of humanitarian activities, and the related costs, are associated with logistics. This is therefore a sector with a high demand for logistics expertise. The available literature and our discussions with representatives of this sector suggest that this expertise is currently lacking. Kovács, Tatham, and Larson (2012) for example refer to "the simultaneous shortage of humanitarian logisticians, high work-force rotation (up to 80 percent per annum) and the challenge of retaining personnel."

Acquiring and retaining the necessary logistics skills in this sector are difficult for several reasons. First, the skills themselves differ from those required by logisticians working in a commercial environment. Local conditions are by definition quite different. Typically, supply chains will have been severely fractured, infrastructure damaged, communication networks disrupted and social and adminstrative services placed under serious strain if not completely eradicated. Yet, despite all this adversity, large, and often traumatized, populations have to be urgently supplied with the basic essentials. This can be logistics at its most challenging. Second, much of the relief agencies' work is concentrated in low and middle income countries where, as discussed earlier, there is already of shortage of logistics skills in the local population. Third, given the resource constraints in this sector, salary levels are often not competitive with those in the business world. Fourth, the risks and rigors of working in disaster zones deters many logistics specialists from switching from the commercial to the humanitarian sector.

In recent years, several studies have examined competency requirements in humanitarian logistics. One central question they have addressed is the extent to which the competencies of the humanitarian logistician differ from the standard range expected of other logistics specialists. Efforts have been made, by Kovács, Tatham, and Larson (2012), Heaslip et al. (2015) and others, to list and classify the humanitarian competencies and try to map them onto the standard competency lists of the major professional associations of logistics. Kovács, Tatham, and Larson (2012), analyzed large samples of job adverts for humanitarian logistics posts to determine what skills and aptitudes the main employers in this sector were looking for. The prevailing view is that most logistics competencies are common to both sectors, though disaster relief operations require specialist training to gain both "contextual" skills and the ability to respond rapidly to unforeseen events. This creates the need for specialist training programs in humanitarian logistics for staff working at different levels in this sector. At the upper managerial level, university programs now exist in several universities such as Lugano, Georgia Tech in Atlanta and Dar-es-Salaam. Charitable foundations, such as the Kuehne Foundation and Fritz Institute, are also active in the development and delivery of training programs in this field.

Within the broader humanitarian logistics world, the HR aspects of the delivery of medical supplies have attracted particular attention. Several initiatives are currently underway to upskill those working in health supply chains in low and middle income countries. An initiative called *People that Deliver* (PtD) was established in 2011 to *"build global and national capacity to implement evidence-based approaches to plan, finance, develop, support and retain the national workforces needed for the effective, efficient and sustainable management of health supply chains"* (www.peoplethatdeliver.org). PtD has developed a three-level training model for healthcare logistics, defining domains, competence areas and behavioral competencies, to assist the development of training programs. It has also created an online platform, called Laptop, where those working in health supply chains can find relevant training material and courses (http://www.rhsupplies.org/activities-resources/tools/laptop/). Other organizations active in this sector are GAVI, the global vaccine and immunizations alliance, and the International Association of Healthcare Professionals. GAVI is currently working with the Gates Foundation, UNICEF and UPS to pilot a new training program in Rwanda for those engaged in the delivery of vaccines. This joint initiative is discussed in "Examples of Best Practices in Competence Development" section in chapter 5 as an example of good practice in competence development.

As humanitarian logistics activities are concentrated in parts of the world where logistics skills are generally in short supply and as momentum is building in the humanitarian sector to upgrade these skills, there are potential synergies to be exploited. The formation of multi-stakeholder groups to address the logistics skills shortage in low and middle income countries should include the various organizations currently working to increase the supply of qualified staff for humanitarian and health supply chains. Logistics training is discussed more fully in the next chapter.

References

Anon. 2014a. "Driver Shortage: Enough of the Talk. It's Action Time." *Fleetwatch*, 28 May. http://fleetwatch.co.za/driver-shortage-enough-of-the-talk-its-action-time/ (Accessed October 12, 2015).

Anon. 2014b. "Brazil Forced to Hire Colombian Truckers Due to Labor Shortages." *Latin American Herald Tribune*, 16 March.

Anon. 2015. "How Do You Solve the Truck Driver Shortage." http://www.commercialfleet .org/fleet-management/driver-training/how-do-you-solve-the-truck-driver-shortage, (accessed October 12, 2015).

Cary, N. 2014. "Expanding U.S. Economy Exposes Rising Truck Driver Shortage." *Reuters*, 2 October. http://www.reuters.com/article/2014/10/02/us-usa-trucks-driver-shortage -idUSKCN0HR2KK20141002, (accessed October 12, 2015).

Cassidy, W. B. 2015. *British Government Pledges to Help Reduce UK Truck Driver Shortage*. http://www.joc.com/trucking-logistics/labor/british-government-pledges-help -reduce-uk-truck-driver-shortage_20150320.html, (accessed October 12, 2015).

Dash, D. K. 2011. "Short of Drivers: 15% of Indian Trucks Lie Idle." *The Times of India*, 3 October.

Directorate-General for Internal Policies, European Parliament. 2009. "Shortage of Qualified Personnel in Road Freight Transport." http://www.europarl.europa.eu /RegData/etudes/etudes/join/2009/419101/IPOL-TRAN_ET(2009)419101_EN.pdf.

Global Insight. 2005. *The U.S. Truck Driver Shortage: Analysis and Forecasts*. Report prepared for the American Trucking Associations.

Heaslip, G., M. C. Henry, D. Blackman, and G. Kovacs. 2015. "Logistics Competencies in Humanitarian Aid." Proceedings of the Production and Operations Management (POMS) conference, Washington DC.

Hsu, Tiffany. 2016. "Number of Female Truckers Slides as Women Face Industry Hurdles." https://www.trucks.com/2016/09/28/female-truckers-face-industry-hurdles/

Kemp, E, S. W. Kopp, and E. C. Kemp. 2013. "Take This Job and Shove It: Examining the Influence of Role Stressors and Emotional Exhaustion on Organizational Commitment and Identification in Professional Truck Drivers." *Journal of Business Logistics* 34 (1).

Kilcarr, S., 2015. *No End in Sight for Worsening Driver Shortage*. http://fleetowner.com /fleet-management/no-end-sight-worsening-driver-shortage, (accessed October 11, 2015).

Kovács, G., P. Tatham, and P. Larson. 2012. "What Skills Are Needed to be a Humanitarian Logistician?" *Journal of Business Logistics* 33 (3): 245–58.

Maqutu, A. 2015. "Truck Drivers in Short Supply." *Business Day Live,* 13 October. http://www.bdlive.co.za/business/transport/2015/10/13/truck-drivers-in-short-supply.

Morris, D. Z. 2015. "There's a Slow-rolling Crisis in Trucking Labor—and It's Costing Everyone." *Fortune* 18 May.

Rauwald, C., and N. Schmidt. 2012. "Wanted in Europe: More Truck Drivers." *The Wall Street Journal.* http://www.wsj.com/articles/SB1000087239639044352490457765162429447 5232 (accessed September 16, 2015).

Sheffi, Y. 2015. "What Price Truck Driver Shortages." *Supply Chain @ MIT.* http://supplychainmit.com/2015/08/20/what-price-truck-driver-shortages/ (accessed August 21, 2015).

Soergel, A., 2015. "An Industry Stuck in Neutral." *US News,* 18 Aug.

TCI (Transport Corporation of India). 2015. "Shortage of Truck Drivers Looms' Transport Corporation of India." Transport Corporation of India. http://www.tcil.com/tcil/pdf/print/Shortage%20of%20Truck%20Drivers%20Looms%20Large.pdf, (accessed October 12, 2015).

Thielman, S. 2015. "Nevada Clears Self-driving 18-wheeler for Testing on Public Roads." *The Guardian,* May 6.

Van Wassenhove, L. N. 2006. "Humanitarian Aid Logistics: Supply Chain Management in High Gear." *Journal of the Operations Research Society* 57 (5): 475–589.

Weiss, R. 2013. "Germany Wants More Truck Drivers." *Bloomberg Business,* 29 Aug. http://www.bloomberg.com/bw/articles/2013-08-29/germany-wants-more-truck-drivers (accessed October 12, 2015).

CHAPTER 5

Training and Skills Development

Nature and Scale of Logistics Training

Where skills are lacking in the existing workforce, the obvious answer is to increase the level of training. The survey responses indicate that the majority of firms across all regions rely on a mixture of internal and external training (figure 5.1). There is one particular difference between regions, though. Companies in developing countries rely twice as heavily on internal training (17 percent vs. 9 percent) compared to their counterparts in the developed world. Often, however, this internal training is simple "on-the-job-training," meaning that new employees receive quick, superficial advice from more experienced peers. Certainly, the supply of external trainers and agencies is greater in the developed world than in developing markets. Nevertheless, there are a significant and expanding training capabilities in less developed countries. CILT has a strong presence and membership network in Sub-Saharan Africa and South-East Asia. CSCMP has been active in Latin America for decades. Even smaller, Western-based training agencies have expanded into low and middle income countries. MGCM for example, a French training agency, designs training courses specifically for Tunisia.

While many companies engage in logistics training activities, survey participants and interviewees from developing regions emphasized that they are dissatisfied with the hours allocated and the quality and the variety of logistics training courses offered by employers (figures 5.2 and 5.3). Almost twice as many respondents from developed countries agreed that they receive a sufficient amount of training time (25 percent vs. 14 percent) and that the training topics vary sufficiently (25 percent vs. 12 percent). Surveyed statistics rely on personal perception and the word "sufficient" is, therefore, quite subjective. However, the numerical data was backed up by the comments of the interviewed experts. According to several anecdotes, "training hours" for warehouse staff in developing countries sometimes consist of simple instructions by the supervisor on how to drive a forklift or where to store and retrieve goods.

Figure 5.1 Sources of Training

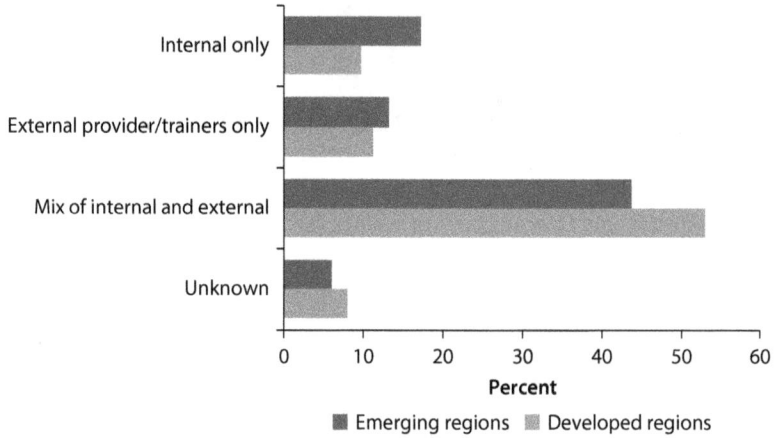

Figure 5.2 Time Allocation to Training

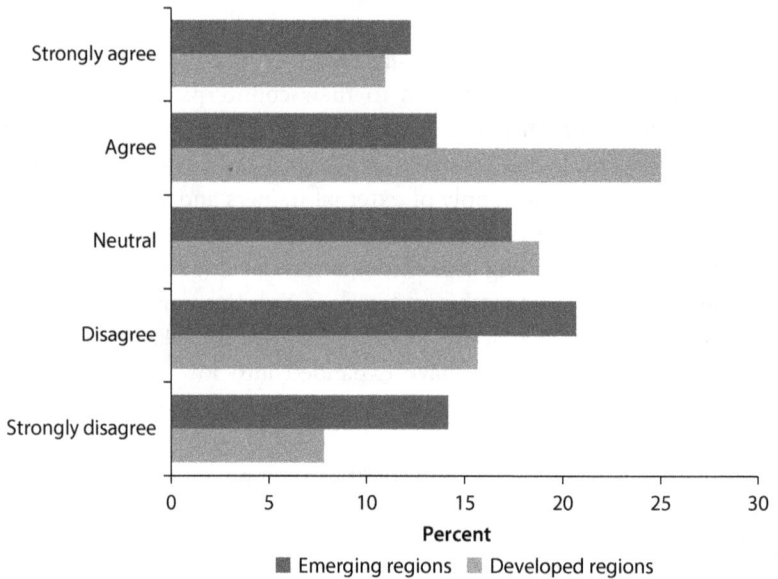

Our consultations revealed a serious gap between developed and developing markets in the provision of logistics training at all occupational levels.

Interviewees argued that the quality and quantity of training are strongly related to firm size and resources, and therefore implicitly to the market structure of the regional logistics sector. In many countries, both higher and lower income ones, a large proportion of trucking operations are sub-contracted by the larger logistics companies to owner-drivers or small carriers with two to five trucks. These logistical small- and medium-sized enterprises (SMEs) cannot afford to design training schemes or sacrifice potential working hours to train their staff.

Figure 5.3 Variety of Logistics Training

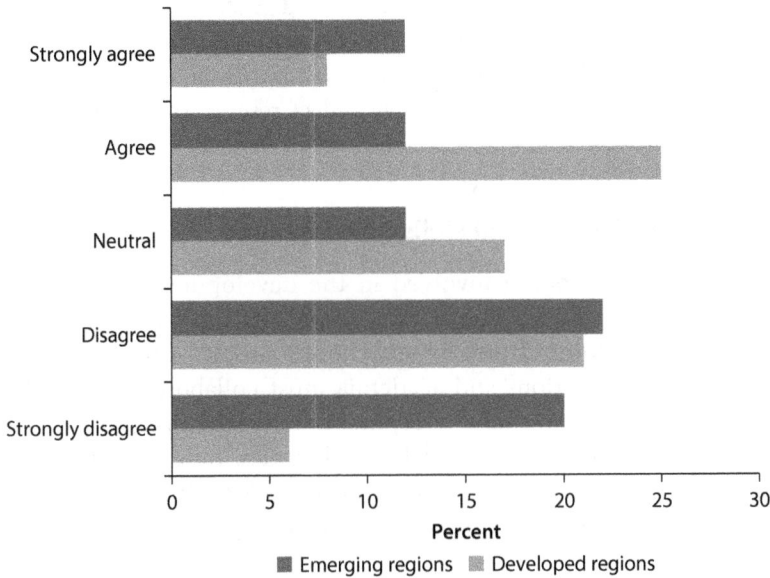

Figure 5.4 Impact of Training on Performance

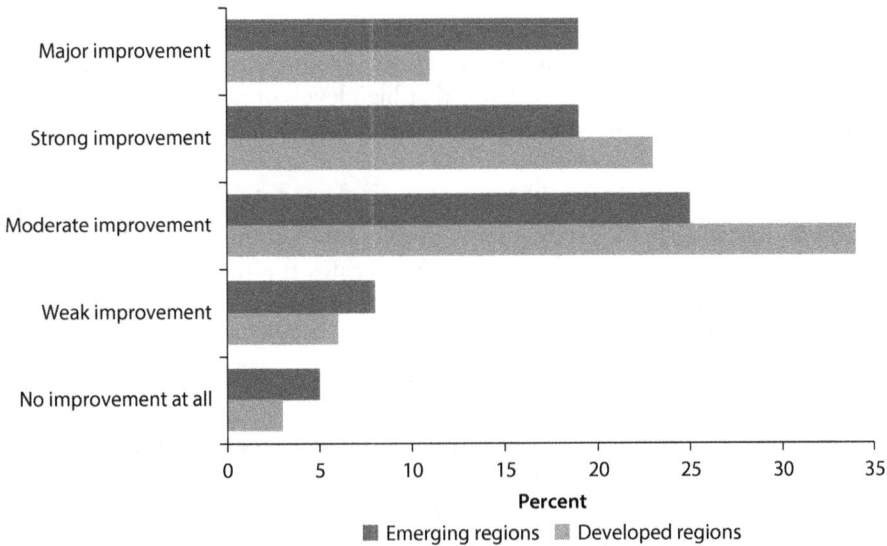

On the other hand, the large 3PLs, though much better resourced, are naturally reluctant to train their sub-contractors' employees, despite the fact that they indirectly suffer from under-skilling of the subcontract workforce.

There has been a tendency for some companies to see training as a cost rather than investment, partly because they have difficulty in quantifying the returns. The survey results show that investment in training capacity is regarded as being both managerially and economically beneficial (figure 5.4). The vast majority of respondents answered that training activities ultimately lead to moderate-to-strong improvements in their company's logistics and SCM performance. A larger proportion of respondents in emerging (developing) regions (19 percent) believe that training can lead to major performance improvement. The bunching of responses in the moderate category may reflect reservations about the quality and relevance of some of the logistics training.

Stakeholders in Training and Skills Development

Numerous stakeholders are involved in the development, monitoring and certification of logistics skills. The majority of the interviewees highlighted the importance of joint efforts by stakeholder groups. Companies, governments, logistics associations and academia must collaborate to identify and exchange best practice in skill development. In less mature logistics markets, they must work together to develop a logistics training capability that can equip the employees on the different occupational levels with the necessary range of skills. Each stakeholder group can perform a different—but complementary—role.

Companies: Our expert panels agreed that the main responsibility for training and developing logistics staff lies in the hands of employers. Companies—both multi-national and local—should have an intrinsic motivation to develop their workforce at all levels. Well-educated, trained employees will pay back the investment in the form of higher levels of productivity and performance. Academic studies have found evidence that high levels of SCM competence and knowledge lead to sustained competitive advantage (Hult et al. 2006; Ellinger et al. 2012).

Companies must decide which employees need to be enrolled in training programs, particularly those designed for logistics staff at the operational, administrative and supervisory levels. Figure 5.5 indicates the relative importance of subject areas for training as rated by respondents to the online survey from developed and developing economies. Almost all the topics received significantly greater support from developing country respondents. While this is a positive finding, it requires careful interpretation.

One possible reason for the lower average percentages assigned to core logistics subjects, such as inventory management, transportation, and warehouse management, by respondents from developed regions is that they expect many of their graduate-level recruits from specialist logistics degree courses to be familiar with these topics. It is also possibly due to a higher degree of specialization in developed countries, resulting in respondents prioritizing training in the core activity of their business, such as transport or warehousing. In developing markets, there is greater variation in the average importance ratings of the subject areas: softer skills like foreign languages, legal issues and supply chain security receive very low scores. The responses from developed countries were much more balanced, suggesting greater recognition of the contribution that these softer skills can make.

Figure 5.5 Training Content

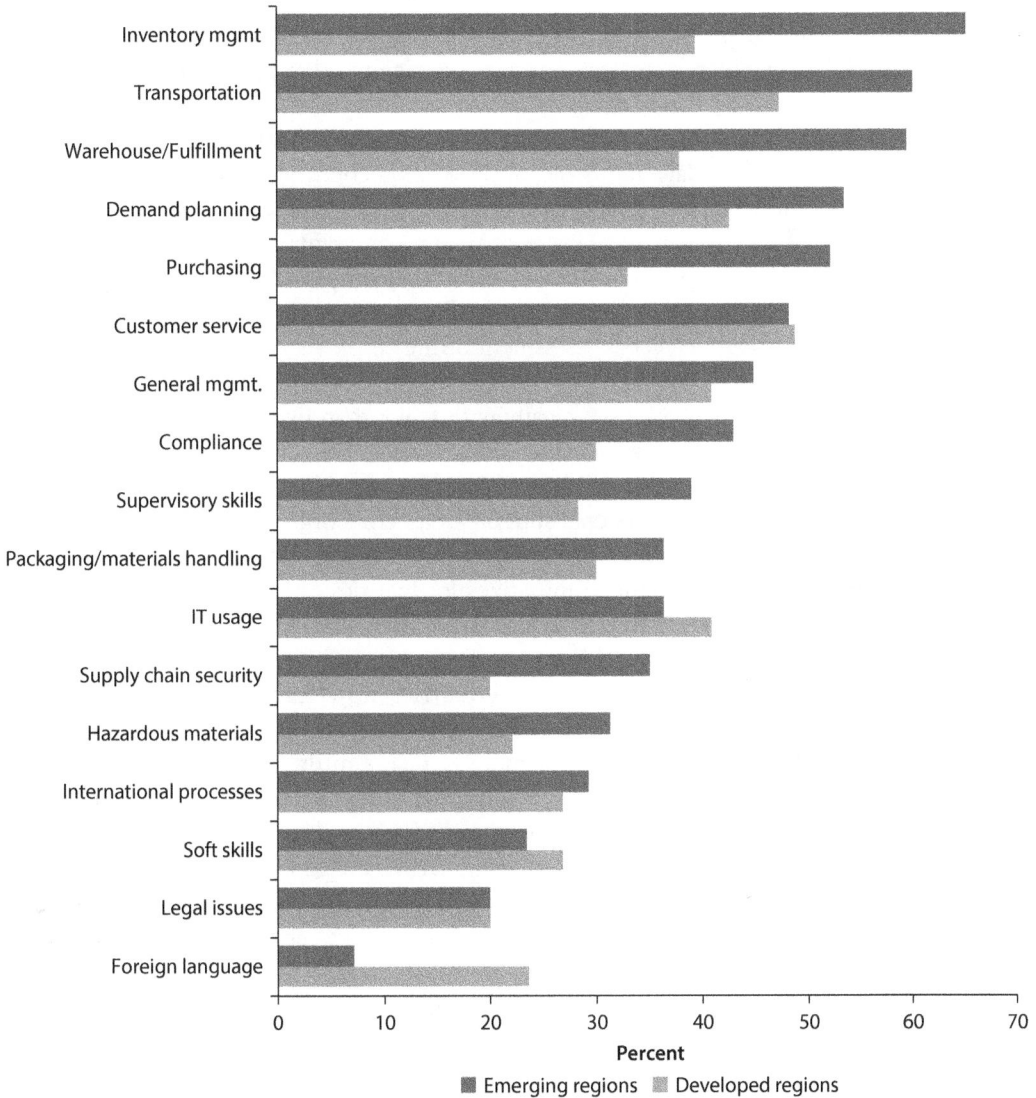

If companies in developing regions want to keep up with international standards, they must complement the current emphasis on the core logistics skills in inventory, warehousing and transport management with training in the broader range of competencies needed to manage complex supply chains with high levels of digitalization and customer expectation. The administrative staff must develop their communication skills, and logistics supervisors and managers must acquire more leadership skills.

Multi-national vs. local firms. Training program maturity is highly correlated with company size. Well-resourced multi-national 3PLs like DHL, DB Schenker and Kühne+Nagel use integrated corporate training programs that combine centralized programs for senior management with regional and local training activities for lower-tier employees. Their *per capita* training budgets are generous by comparison with those of local businesses, particularly in the trucking and warehousing sectors. Several interviewees claimed that the logistics staff in small companies—especially in operational roles—are expected to generate revenues from day one of their employment. Competition is so intense in the highly fragmented road haulage industries of developing countries that truck drivers must be on the road every day. Thus many haulage businesses lack the necessary budget and/or expertise to instigate training programs.

Concerns were also raised about the quality and utility of the training programs currently in place. Many small companies in the logistics sector do not undertake a proper needs assessment of the employees to be trained and simply use pre-existing training materials, regardless of whether or not they are relevant. These smaller companies, typically with fewer than five vehicles, form the backbone of a country's logistics operations and can collectively be responsible for a much higher share of freight movement than the larger players. Companies like these require the professional support of external organizations. In order to raise their competence level, multi-national companies could be incentivized to support industry-wide training initiatives for logistics SMEs. Since the larger 3PLs sub-contract much of their haulage to these smaller operators, they would indirectly benefit from this wider up-skilling.

Logistics associations: Many countries now have professional associations for logistics. The three largest ones, CILT (United Kingdom), CSCMP (United States) and BVL (Germany), have a multi-national presence and a critical role to play in the development, assessment and certification of professional standards in logistics and SCM worldwide. In Europe, many of the national associations, including CILT and BVL, are affiliated to the European Logistics Association (ELA), which co-ordinates professional development efforts on a continental level and represents logistics in governmental and industry forums. International and national logistics associations offer training programs and qualifications that they deliver through multiple channels. The major associations have a large, diverse membership base which is kept updated on developments in the field and training initiatives through conferences, webinars and newsletters.

Several lower-income countries such as Oman, Jordan, Argentina, Peru and Uruguay have national logistics associations.[1] Efforts have been made by the World Bank and International Finance Corporation to set up a Logistics Association in the Arab Republic of Egypt, a country in which there is no established locus for institutional responsibility for logistics. Among other activities, this association would have organized logistics training courses. Unfortunately the initiative was unsuccessful due to a lack of funding.

Many associations offer a variety of training materials, training programs and professional trainers. Their programs range from comprehensive logistics degrees that require several years of study to short workshops and independent online courses. Logistics companies can benefit from logistics association membership in several ways. Attendance at meetings and conferences allows members to accumulate continuing professional development (CPD) credits. CILT defines CPD as the "systematic maintenance and improvement of knowledge, skills and competence throughout a professional's working life." Members of the association are encouraged to develop CPD plans and to accumulate CPD credits, which are used to assess their suitability for higher levels of membership. Appendix B contains an example of a CPD plan.

Professional associations relieve individual companies of the need to design and facilitate their own training courses and materials. They also provide standardized assessment and certification of the skills acquired through training. In addition, they maintain high levels of quality in the courses they deliver themselves and the ones offered by the other agencies and institutions that they accredit. The qualifications and certificates they award to successful students and companies are highly reputable and recognized globally.

The vast majority of survey respondents believe that professional logistics associations have essential/important roles and responsibilities in promoting careers in logistics and SCM (figure 5.6). A significantly higher share of the respondents in developing regions deemed the role of the associations to be essential. These survey findings were in line with the interview comments received. Western-based associations have been responding to the strong demand for professionalized logistics in developing economies. CILT International, for instance, has a large footprint in Africa—as reflected by the large number of member countries and companies. The collaboration between national and international logistics associations facilitates the transfer of state-of-the-art logistics knowledge from developed countries to developing ones and the standardization of logistics competencies worldwide. There is also collaboration between professional associations: for example, between CILT and APICS. While CILT has greater expertise and more extensive networking in the transport sector, APICS is an SCM-oriented association. Depending on the clients' needs, the associations can jointly provide training, dividing their input

Figure 5.6 Role of Logistics Associations

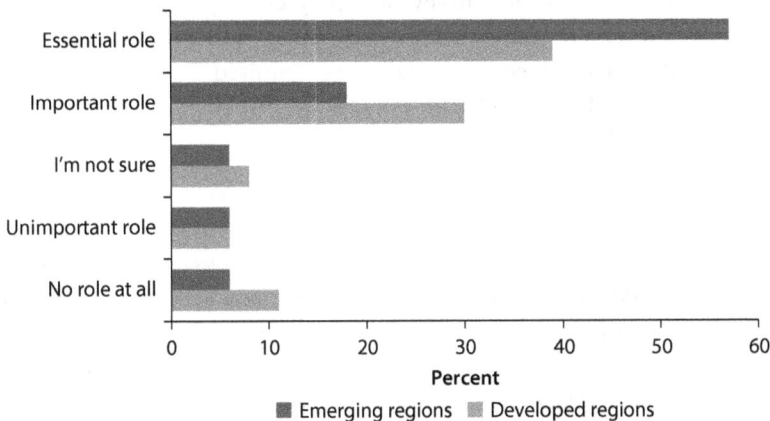

in line with their core competencies. The activities of the large professional logistics associations are outlined in greater detail in "Examples of Best Practices in Competence Development" section in chapter 5.

Higher education: Colleges, universities and vocational schools provide the foundation for future logistics leadership. These institutions are responsible for the education of logistics managers at the upper end of the educational hierarchy. Over the last few decades, many universities have launched specialist bachelor and master programs in logistics and SCM and/or incorporated logistics/SCM modules into other, more general management-focused curricula. Some of this university and college level provision has been funded by governments in recognition of logistics' role as an essential enabler of economic growth and wealth (Korn 2013). However, as indicated by our survey results, higher educational programs across all regions have not been producing enough young logistics professionals to meet market demand. According to our interviewees, this is not the only concern. They have suggested that, particularly in developing regions, not only the quantity but also the quality of the academic logistics education is sub-optimal. The interviewees emphasized that in some countries, such as Thailand and Brazil, the number of people holding a logistics degree is adequate on paper, but unfortunately, graduates do not possess the skills or the knowledge required in practice. As a consequence, positions are held by unqualified staff or left vacant despite the large number of applicants.

Holcomb, Krul, and Thomas (2015) and many interviewees argued that academia and industry must collaborate more closely to ensure that the next generation of logistics/SCM graduates is equipped with the skill sets required by practice. Unfortunately, the content taught in colleges and universities in developing economies is often outdated. Interviewees noted that some regional colleges in China and Thailand still use teaching materials from the 1980s in their lectures today. The lecturing styles in these countries were also criticized for often relying solely on traditional lecture-style instruction. More modern didactic approaches are required to imbue students with important practical skills such as communication, teamwork, presentation, project management and negotiation. The criticism of course content and delivery was not confined to developing economies, however. A recent survey of supply chain professionals—mainly in the developed world—revealed that they also find it difficult to recruit graduates from universities who have the skill sets required in practice (Logistics Management 2011). The 2014 SCM World Survey of chief supply chain officers concluded that:

> Since 2011, when we first started surveying supply chain practitioners on talent management, the pressure has ramped up steadily. Despite rising interest in supply chains among universities and significant investments by professional associations such as APICS, the ISM and the CSCMP, business leaders seem to be facing harder times building and managing their teams than ever before. In fact, 43% of supply chain practitioners say that this task has become harder in the past two years—nearly double the rate in 2011 and up notably over last year. (O'Marah et al. 2014, p. 30)

The specialists interviewed for the present study suggested several remedies:

Firstly, universities in developing economies should partner with well-established institutions in developed countries to initiate a knowledge transfer and obtain advice on how to adopt up-to-date teaching methods. Examples are presented in "Examples of Best Practices in Competence Development" section in chapter 5. Secondly, Western universities could expand their intake of students from developing countries into logistics/SCM programs. This usually gives them access to state-of-the-art education and equips them with knowledge and skills to take back to their home countries. There is always the risk, of course, that these students find employment locally and do not return to their home countries. The United Kingdom, the United States, Australia and, to a lesser extent, Germany, the Netherlands and Sweden, already attract many students from developing markets to their logistics programs, despite relatively high tuition and living costs. The current financial barrier to studying at Western universities could be eased for the most promising candidates if the hosting universities, the home country's government or third parties awarded more scholarships. Finally, American and European professors could possibly do more to support the development of logistics and SCM courses in emerging markets. At an institutional level, MIT has successfully established logistics institutes in Colombia and Malaysia, as discussed in greater detail in "Examples of Best Practices in Competence Development" section in chapter 5.

Our consultations suggest that universities in developed countries are better at improving students' soft skills, particularly in the areas of leadership, communication and cross-cultural management, where, according to our surveys. There are currently competence deficits. As discussed earlier, sometimes the reasons for deficiencies in communication and leadership have cultural roots.

While universities and colleges educate future managers and senior administrative staff, vocational schools play a key role in preparing staff for operational and supervisory jobs and helping them climb the career ladder. In contrast to academic institutions (universities and colleges), vocational schools or private academies focus on teaching practical, applicable skills rather than theoretical concepts. Their training programs typically have more practical content and give students more hands-on experience through internships and work assignments. This requires close collaboration between companies and vocational schools/academies. The collaboration with industry is well exemplified by the dual-education approach that is long-established in Germany. This is one of the many examples of best practice in logistics competence development discussed in the next section.

Examples of Best Practices in Competence Development

Numerous examples of best practice in logistics training and competence development were identified. This section examines a selection that appears to be working well in practice.

Associations of logistics professionals: Our review of the training, accreditation and certification activities of the larger associations revealed examples of best practice that smaller, nationally-based associations would do well to emulate. Survey respondents felt that professional associations should play an essential role in promoting logistics and upgrading logistics skills.

Chartered Institute of Logistics and Transport (CILT): CILT's training programs give transport and logistics practitioners a strong foundation for their career development. With five levels of qualification available from school-leaver to graduate level, learning with CILT can take place flexibly and at the candidate's own pace. The qualifications are recognized globally and enable students to advance their careers as they work their way through the various levels. The full range of CILT courses can be accessed through classroom teaching, distance learning and e-learning formats. Many of them have a modular structure. For employers, this is a promising way to ensure that the staff are well trained in the basics of supply chain management, logistics and transport, using the course options that best match the needs of the business. The course content and qualifications have been tailored to the needs of logistics and transport businesses around the world. Each qualification is assessed against lists of key knowledge areas and competencies that are regularly reviewed by teams of academics and practitioners (CILT 2015a).

European Logistics Association (ELA): ELA is a federation of thirty national logistics organizations covering almost all of Europe. The ELA Standards of Logistics Competence were developed with and agreed by the logistics industry. The ELA Standards are outcome-based and form the basis of the assessment, which is independent of any learning program. ELA certification is widely recognized throughout Europe and beyond. This offers flexibility to certified logistics employees seeking employment in different European countries. Assessment is available from the ELA National Certification Boards established in more than 20 countries. An ELA certificate recognizes competencies and validates logisticians' experience at different levels (ELA 2015).

APICS—The Association for Operations Management: APICS is a professional association for supply chain and operations management and a provider of research, education and certification programs that "aim to elevate supply chain excellence, innovation and resilience." APICS has 43,000 members and more than 30 international partners. It offers three main certificates and an endorsement: certificate in production and inventory management (CPIM), certified supply chain professional (CSCP), certified fellow in production and inventory management (CFPIM) and SCOR professional endorsement (SCOR-P). For example, someone with a CSCP qualification would be expected to have the knowledge and organizational skills needed to manage supply chain operations. It is the most widely recognized international educational program for operations and supply chain management professionals. Since its launch in 2006, more than 17,000 professionals in 82 countries have earned the APICS CSCP designation. (APICS 2015).

In addition to the main logistics associations operating at a global scale, there are many established associations at the country level: for example, BVL in Germany, AILOG in Italy, or CEL in Spain. Many of them exhibit best practice in the derivation, marketing and implementation of professional standards.

Industry Associations

International Road Transport Union (IRU): IRU is the trade organization which represents the interests of commercial road transport businesses worldwide, including those operating freight vehicles. Its "training arm," the IRU Academy, offers a "portfolio of training programs to road transport professionals through its global network of Accredited Training Institutes (ATIs)" in over 50 countries. It is committed to raising professional standards in the road freight sector and gaining professional recognition for those working in the industry. The organization's programs "integrate best practices and guarantee compliance with applicable international, EU and national regulations in order to meet the objective of harmonizing training standards at a global level." In addition to providing training materials for delivery by the ATIs to the road freight workforce, the IRU also helps to enhance the capability of the ATIs by running "Train the Trainer" sessions. This helps to ensure the quality of the training provided. The IRU's general courses lead to the award of certificates of professional competence (CPC) at both managerial and driver levels and are supplemented by specialist courses, *inter alia*, on the transport of dangerous goods, cargo security and eco-driving. ATIs receive packages comprising lesson plans, presentations, simulations, videos, glossaries and as well as assessment material.

The Advisory Committee of the IRU Academy is composed of representatives of the World Bank, the International Transport Forum, the UN, the European Commission and the European Transport Workers Federation. It has a separate Accreditation Committee responsible for the maintenance of professional standards across its training network.

FIATA Logistics Academy: FIATA is the International Federation of Freight Forwarding Associations which represents "an industry covering approximately 40,000 forwarding and logistics firms employing around 8–10 million people in 150 countries." It set up its Logistics Academy in 2014 to "add value to FIATA members by positioning training, development and research in freight logistics as a priority to provide a sustainable, quality management facility for professional training to FIATA members (…) to promote collaboration and mutual recognition with international, national and regional bodies and to enhance access to careers in supply chain management." Its training is geared towards the managerial level. The Academy works with a group of partner universities and relies heavily on online delivery of training modules to employees in the freight forwarding sector, drawing where possible on existing material. It has arranged for a suite of management MOOCs[2] prepared by edX at Harvard Business School to be available managers in the freight forwarding sector, but is also in the process of developing new modules in specific aspects of forwarding, such as the safety and security of goods in transit. The Logistics Academy supplements FIATA's long established training schemes for apprentices in the freight forwarding sector.

International branch campuses: The Massachusetts Institute of Technology (MIT) has established a Center for Latin American Logistics Innovation (CLI) in Bogota, Colombia. The SCALE Latin America flagship student program, the most extensive of its type in Latin America, leads to the award of the Graduate Certificate in Logistics and Supply Chain Management (GCLOG). The GCLOG program started in July 2009. Presented by the MIT Center for Transportation and Logistics (CTL) faculty, the program's goal is to train aspiring logistics and supply chain professionals in the region. MIT CTL and CLI have cultivated close relationships with 27 Latin American universities. The SCALE Network is used to provide opportunities for academics in the region to improve the teaching methods and program content in the supply chain field at their local universities. They achieve this through a series of English-language academic workshops that take place annually at various venues across Latin America. An integral part of CLI activities in the region is collaboration with corporate partners. To date, CLI has 12 strategic corporate partners (MIT 2015). More recently MIT has extended its SCALE network into East Asia with the establishment of the Malaysia Institute for Supply Chain Innovation (MISI).

Georgia Tech has founded a logistics innovation and research center in Panama. It is the latest addition to the Georgia Tech Supply Chain & Logistics Institute (SCL). Under an agreement negotiated with Panama's National Secretariat of Science, Technology and Innovation, SCL undertakes research and education in logistics and trade. The center's strategic objectives are to improve the logistics performance of the country and help develop its logistics and trade capabilities, thus enabling Panama to become the trade hub of the Americas (Georgia Tech University 2015).

The renowned German university RWTH Aachen has opened a campus in Oman: the German University of Technology (GUtech). A focus group participant from Oman noted that this initiative is well received by Oman companies and its graduates are the first choice for filling entry-level positions. The BSc in Logistics combines an education in business and general management with an introduction to the fields of logistics and supply chain management. It provides solid, in-depth knowledge of logistics, supply chain management and transportation management. The program is tailored to the requirements of the Sultanate of Oman and the region, but draws on the state-of-the-art expertise accumulated at RWTH Aachen.

The program puts a strong emphasis on the employability of GUtech graduates. For this reason, many of the program's elements are taught in cooperation with local and international industry partners. Generic skills such as critical thinking, creativity, life-long learning, intercultural communication and teamwork are considered essential and are thus integrated into the curriculum. A faculty based in Muscat and visiting professors from RWTH Aachen and other renowned universities teach the courses. The language of instruction is English, including written and oral tests, seminar papers and the bachelor's thesis. Students are also expected to develop communication skills in German (GUtech 2015).

Another example of best-practice in education and multi-stakeholder facilitation is The Logistics Institute—Asia Pacific (TLI—Asia Pacific) in Singapore. Established in 1998 under the Global School House Program, TLI—Asia Pacific is a collaboration between National University of Singapore and Georgia Tech for research and educational programs in global logistics. The Institute provides postgraduate and executive education in logistics and SCM. Since its inception, it has served as the training ground for aspiring logisticians, equipping them with analytical tools to meet supply chain challenges. A particularly important function is to bring together government, universities and industry in logistics in Singapore. The Institute hosts a regular series of so-called THINK forums that bring thought-leaders in research and industry together to discuss contemporary SCM issues, challenges and solutions.

Dual education and apprenticeship programs: Germany, Austria and Switzerland have embraced the industry-linked vocational school system for several hundred years. Its apprenticeship system has been recognized as one of the key sources of Germany's economic strength and world leadership in engineering and other technical sectors, including logistics. Italy and Spain have recently adopted the German dual education system and it has also been recommended for adoption by the UK logistics sector (Skills for Logistics 2014a). Due to the combination of theoretical lessons in vocational schools and practical education on the company side, the gap between theory and practice is bridged quickly and efficiently. Apprenticeships foster job-related skills that can be rapidly put into action when the candidate takes up a full-time post. As shown in figure 5.7, countries with a high percentage of vocational education tend to have lower youth unemployment rates than countries with a low level of vocational education. Furthermore, apprentices are often educated so comprehensively that they are not only prepared for their entry-level job, but also for future leadership positions higher on the career ladder.

As one part of the dual education system, the employing company trains students three to five days a week. The companies are responsible for ensuring that students receive a minimum quality and quantity of training. Students also attend vocational schools (German: "Berufsschule") for approximately 60 days a year, often organized in blocks of one or two weeks distributed over the year. The program is usually completed in 2.5–3 years by passing mandatory exams. Since apprenticeship systems require companies to invest significant sums in young employees, in Germany businesses commonly agree to refrain from poaching current or recently graduated apprentices from competitors. In an effort to reduce the upfront investment in apprenticeship systems, developing countries could try to reduce their duration from two years to six months for certain tasks that require lower levels of training and experience.

The BiS-Henderson Academy is a good best practice example of a private apprenticeship system developed in cooperation with companies. It offers a job in an SCM and logistics skills development program designed by the employing company itself. This provides a "framework" containing a number of separately

Figure 5.7 Dual Education and Youth Unemployment

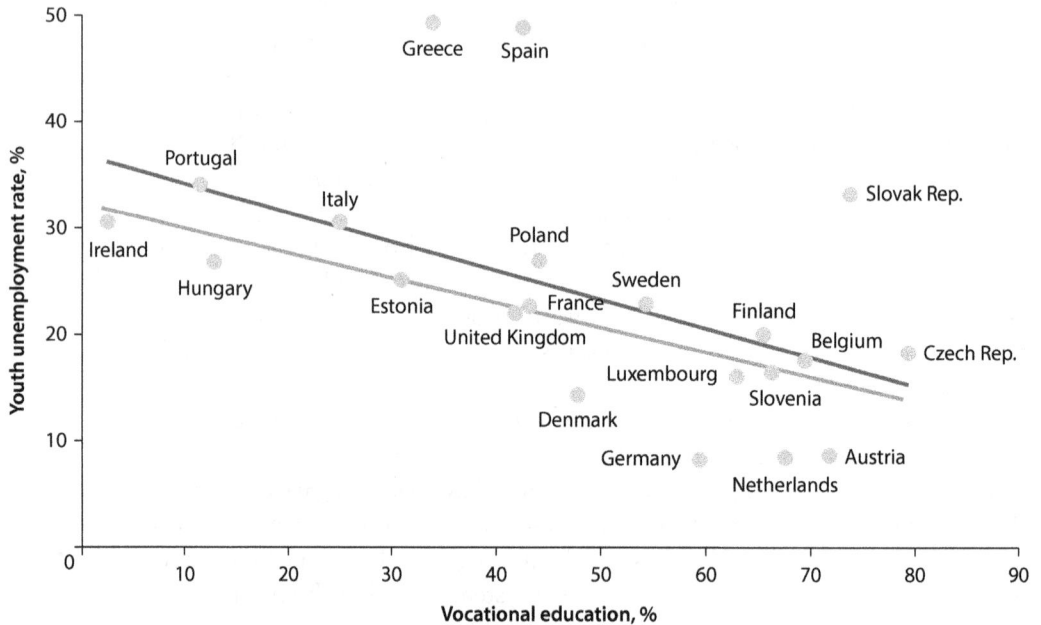

Sources: OECD 2008, Education at a Glance 2008; Eurostat. Adapted from Hanushek 2012.

certified qualifications and courses that cover the skills, competencies and basic knowledge required for this specific job (BiS-Henderson Academy 2015).

Joint university/industry development of a logistics bachelors program: The Novus program at the University of Huddersfield in the United Kingdom shows how industry can take a proactive role in the development of a bachelor-level logistics course (University of Huddersfield 2015). In recognition of the need to increase the flow of well-qualified logistics/SCM graduates, a group of UK-based companies coordinated by BIS-Henderson approached several UK universities with a proposal to support the development of a degree program. The University of Huddersfield, which was the first university in the United Kingdom to enter the undergraduate market in logistics education back in the 1980s, was selected and the Novus program was born. The program has proved very popular with students. It has several distinguishing features:

- All students graduating with at least an upper second class degree are guaranteed a graduate-level supply chain/logistics job with one of the sponsoring companies.
- The program has been designed in partnership with these companies.
- During the program, students complete paid internships with the companies over the summer months and have a full year internship during the third year of the program.

- Company managers lead seminars and host site visits.
- Each student has a company mentor for the duration of the program.

Hands-on learning experience: Despite the fact that a sound theoretical education is essential to understanding business processes, logistics employees acquire much of the required knowledge and skill set through practical application. While this happens automatically on the job, experiential learning approaches such as business games are useful tools for teaching and simulating logistics processes without being exposed to the risk of making costly mistakes in a real company.

The McKinsey & Company Model Warehouse is a good example of how simulation can be used in a simple, affordable and hands-on way. It shows how warehouse operations can be designed and managed. The experiential learning approach enables logistics staff from all levels to experience warehouse processes and improvement levers in one- to several-day workshops (figure 5.8). By using scaled

Figure 5.8 Hands-On Learning Experience: McKinsey & Company Model Warehouse

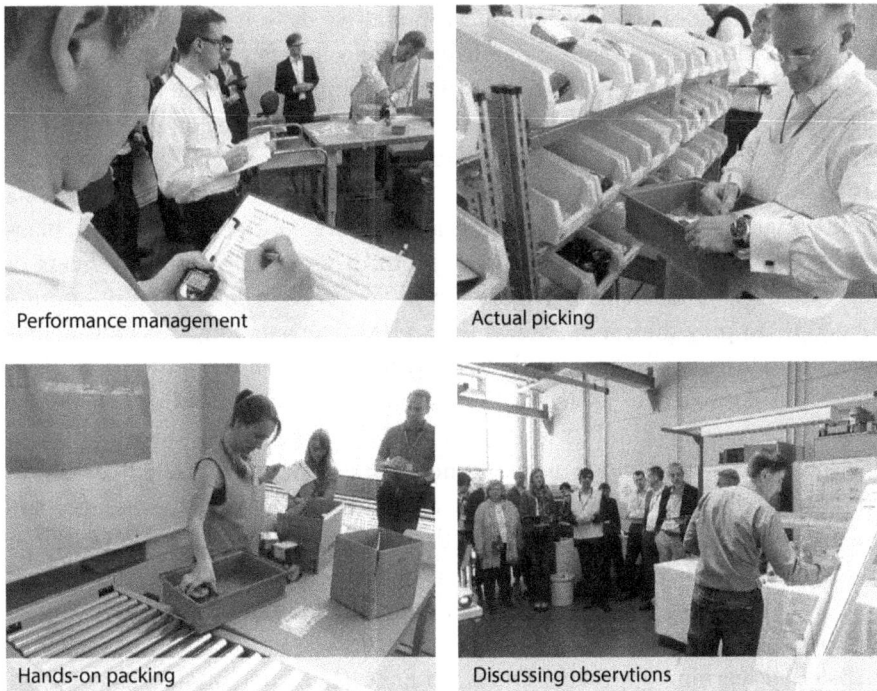

Performance management

Actual picking

Hands-on packing

Discussing observtions

Source: © McKinsey & Company. Used with permission; further permission required for reuse. http://capability-center
.mckinsey.com/lean-warehousing.
Note: The McKinsey Model Warehouse is a great example for a simple and affordable way to simulate typical warehouse operations hands-on. The experiential learning approach enables logistics staff from all levels to experience warehouse processes and improvement levers in one to several day workshops. By using scaled down warehouse equipment and items, a standard warehouse environment is modeled on a few square meters of space. The equipment can be fitted into a small container and shipped around the globe easily to teach logistics staff at any location. Capabilities developed in a hands-on experiential learning environment such as the model warehouse are retained much longer than knowledge that is obtained by reading, seeing and hearing only (McKinsey & Company 2015).

Figure 5.9 Hands-On Logistics and SCM Business Games

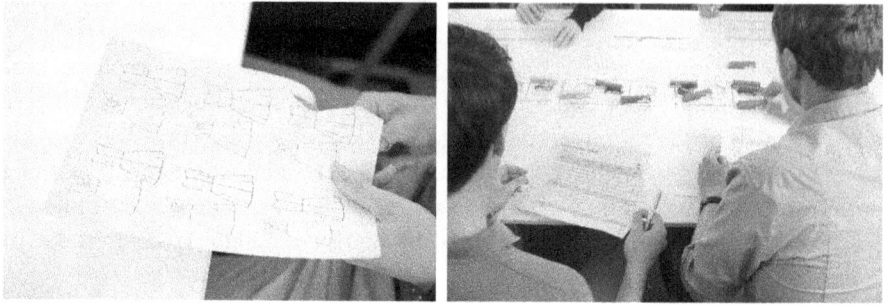

Source: © Kai Hoberg and Christoph Flöthmann / Kühne Logistics University (photographer: Susann Linke). Used with permission; further permission required for reuse.

down warehouse equipment and items, a standard warehouse environment is modeled in a few square meters of space. The equipment can be easily packed in a small container and shipped around the globe to teach logistics staff at any location. The capabilities developed in using a model like this are retained much longer than knowledge that is obtained purely by reading, listening or observing.

Hoberg and Flöthmann (2012) developed a simple, hands-on business game that has been used extensively to teach the "postponement" principle in supply chains to university students, humanitarian logisticians, non-logistics professionals and strategy consultants. Their "Prom Dress Game" simulates a fashion manufacturer. The participants are in charge of the management, planning and production of two different prom dresses, using colored sheets of paper, scissors and staplers (figure 5.9). The cost of material for around 30 people to play the game are less than $100. The game provides a valuable, convincing learning experience that is easy to grasp even without much previous SCM knowledge (teaching slides, etc. are available free of charge at: https://www.the-klu.org/experiential-scm-learning/).

Probably the most widely used business game in this field is the Beer Game. For several decades, it has illustrated the "bullwhip effect" to students and managers (Lau 2015). If uncorrected, the effect can destabilize supply chains and seriously inflate inventory levels and costs. It is vitally important that supply chain managers understand the phenomenon and know how to deal with it.

Blended learning approach: Deutsche Bahn (DB International) is currently developing a comprehensive educational system for railway companies in Saudi Arabia, the UAE and Qatar to transfer its extensive railroad knowledge to countries that are at an earlier stage of railroad development. The teaching approach will rest on three pillars: theory, practice and eLearning. The theoretical pillar consists of traditional classroom sessions to outline the theoretical background for railroad workers. The practical pillar consists of a school for train driving, train maintenance and other related tasks. The third and most innovative pillar consists of an eLearning platform that students can access via their personal smartphones. The eLearning modules and assignments are designed to last 20 minutes, enabling students to work on assignments during short breaks in their daily routines.

Adjustment of curricula, materials and teaching styles to regional needs: In addition to the large logistics associations, there are many smaller recruiting and training agencies that offer continuing education on a commercial basis. Their quality and relevance are difficult to assess, although some of them clearly have a long history of training in this field. For instance, the French-based MGCM has trained 15,000 students from over 2,500 companies over the last 25 years (MGCM 2015). MGCM offers its French-language courses in France and Tunisia. Since blue-collar workers in these countries often lack proficiency in English, offering courses in their native language is certainly a major advantage. As a relatively small organization, MGCM claims that it can be flexible in adjusting curricula to client needs. The company not only offers training in French, but also adjusts the teaching styles to the cultural and local milieu of their clients. For instance, they have found that in India, case studies and practical exercises should be given greater priority than theoretical learning and exams.

Public-private-partnerships (PPP) for joint training programs: The Global Alliance for Vaccines and Immunization (GAVI) is a public-private global health partnership committed to increasing access to immunization in poor countries (Global Alliance for Vaccines and Immunization 2015). A landscape analysis completed last year revealed gaps in both technical and general management competencies among health supply chain leaders. The same analysis discovered that, while sufficient technical competency training is available, there is a lack of training in general leadership—a finding that our survey and interview data confirm. Recognizing that the private sector is a valuable source of guidance on leadership development, GAVI has entered into an innovative public-private relationship with the logistics company UPS to produce a leadership development program that provides health SCM professionals and decision-makers with core leadership and management skills (People that Deliver 2015).

This so-called STEP (Strategic Training Executive Program) program blends instructor-led classroom sessions, distance learning assignments and activity and mentorship opportunities (figure 5.10). It provides instruction in people management, problem solving, communication, project management and professional development. The distance-learning phase is delivered via DVD or online over a 3–6-month period. The instructor-led courses are compressed into a workshop of only 3–4 days that delivers people-management and communication skills. A private sector expert on the subject matter supervises the distance-learning phase and serves as a mentor for the participants' work on practical aspects of the course.

Figure 5.10 GAVI STEP Framework: HR Leadership for Supply Chain Managers

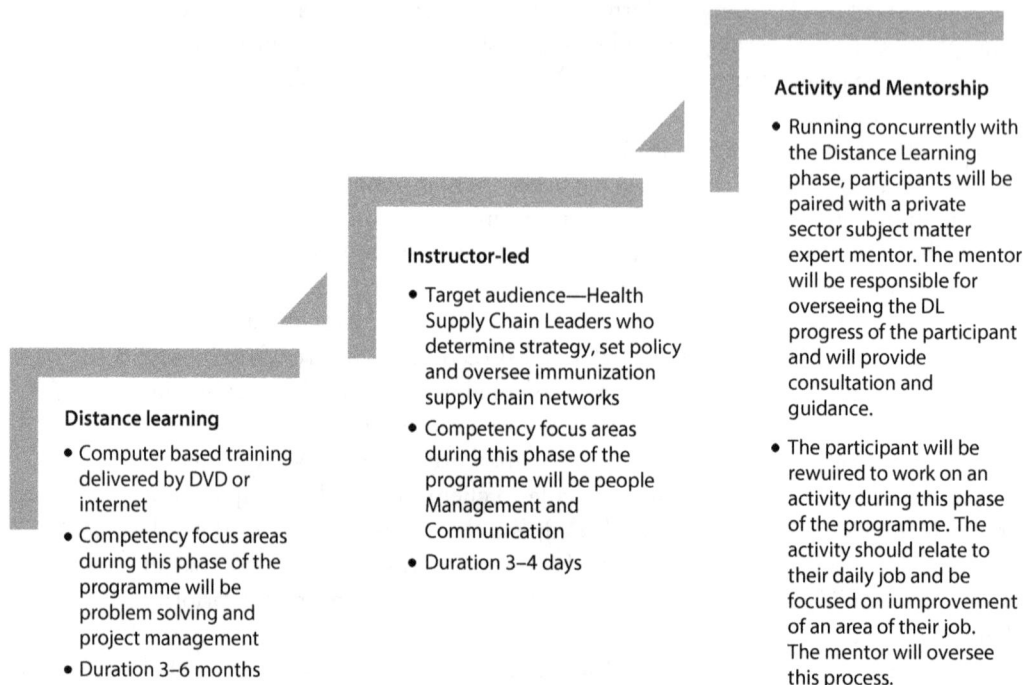

Activity and Mentorship

- Running concurrently with the Distance Learning phase, participants will be paired with a private sector subject matter expert mentor. The mentor will be responsible for overseeing the DL progress of the participant and will provide consultation and guidance.

- The participant will be rewuired to work on an activity during this phase of the programme. The activity should relate to their daily job and be focused on iumprovement of an area of their job. The mentor will oversee this process.

Instructor-led

- Target audience—Health Supply Chain Leaders who determine strategy, set policy and oversee immunization supply chain networks

- Competency focus areas during this phase of the programme will be people Management and Communication

- Duration 3–4 days

Distance learning

- Computer based training delivered by DVD or internet

- Competency focus areas during this phase of the programme will be problem solving and project management

- Duration 3–6 months

Source: © GAVI. Used with permission; further permission required for reuse.

Notes

1. Oman Logistics and Supply Chain Association, Jordanian Logistics Association, Asociación Argentina de logística empresaria, Asociación peruana de profesionales de logística, INALOG (Instituto Nacional de Logística) (Uruguay).

2. A MOOC is a Massive Online Open Course.

References

APICS. 2015. "APICS Certification" (accessed September 17, 2015), http://www.apics .org/careers-education-professional-development/certification.

BiS-Henderson Academy. 2015. "BiS-Henderson Academy" (accessed September 18, 2015), http://www.bis-hendersonacademy.com/the-academy/.

CILT. 2015a. "CILT Certification" (accessed September 17, 2015), http://www.ciltinter national.org/education-development/why-learn-with-us/.

ELA. 2015. "Concept of the ELA Certification" (accessed September 17, 2015), http:// www.elalog.eu/concept-ela-certification.

Ellinger, A. E., H. Shin, W. M. Northington, F. G. Adams, D. Hofman, and K. O'Marah. 2012. "The Influence of Supply Chain Management Competency on Customer Satisfaction and Shareholder Value." *Supply Chain Management: An International Journal* 17 (3): 249–62.

Georgia Tech University. 2015. Georgia Tech Panama Logistics Innovation & Research Center (accessed September 17, 2015), http://www.gatech.pa/en/.

Global Alliance for Vaccines and Immunization. 2015. "About Gavi" (accessed September 12, 2015), http://www.gavi.org/about/.

GUtech. 2015. "GUtech BSc in Logistics" (accessed September 18, 2015), http://www.gutech.edu.om/academic/business-economics/logistics/.

Hanushek, E. A. 2012. "Dual Education : Europe's Secret Recipe?" *CESifo Forum* 3: 29–34.

Hoberg, K., and C. Flöthmann. 2012. "Experiential Learning for Humanitarian Logistics." In *Humanitarian Logistics in Asia-Pacific: Challenges, Opportunities and Perspectives,* edited by R. de Souza and J. Stumpf, Kühne Foundation Book Series on Logistics 19. Haupt Publisher.

Holcomb, M., A. Krul, and D. Thomas. 2015. "Supply Chain Talent Squeeze: How Business and Universities Are Collaborating to Fill the Gap." *Supply Chain Management Review* (July/August): 10–19.

Hult, G.T.M., D. J. Ketchen Jr., S. T. Cavusgil, and R. J. Calantone. 2006. "Knowledge as a Strategic Resource in Supply Chains." *Journal of Operations Management* 24: 458–75.

Korn, M. 2013. "The Hot New M.B.A.: Supply-Chain Management" (accessed November 11, 2015), http://www.wsj.com/articles/SB10001424127887324423904578523591792789054.

Lau, A. 2015. "Teaching Supply Chain Management using a Modified Beer Game: An Action Learning Approach." *International Journal of Logistics: Research and Applications* 18 (1): 62–81.

Logistics Management. 2011. "Logistics Management." 27th Annual Salary Survey: Ready to Move Up (accessed September 11, 2015), http://www.logisticsmgmt.com/article/27th_annual_salary_survey_ready_to_move_up/.

MGCM. 2015. "MGCM" (Accessed September 21, 2015), http://www.mgcm.com/en/welcome.

MIT. 2015. "MIT Global SCALE Network" (Accessed September 18, 2015), http://scale.mit.edu/centers/center-latin-american-logistics-innovation.

OECD (Organisation for Economic Co-operation and Development). 2008. *Education at a Glance 2008.* Paris: OECD.

O'Marah, K., G. John, B. Blake, and P. Manenti. 2014. *The Chief Supply Chain Officer Report 2014.* SCM World, ed., London.

People that Deliver. 2015. "Health Supply Chain Competency Framework for Managers & Leaders." http://www.peoplethatdeliver.org/.

Skills for Logistics. 2014a. "Apprenticeships" (accessed October 20, 2015), http://www.skillsforlogistics.org/qualifications-training/apprenticeships/.

University of Huddersfield. 2015. "Novus" (accessed October 19, 2015), https://www.hud.ac.uk/uhbs/novus.

CHAPTER 6

Recruitment and Retention

Recruitment

The global shortage of qualified personnel is putting additional pressure on recruitment processes and strategies. Companies have been fighting the "war for talent" for years. The aging population in the Western world and more specifically, the retirement of the baby-boom generation, will widen the gap between labor supply and demand across the logistics sector in the near future. Logistics companies are not only competing with each other but also with other sectors to attract young professionals into the industry. The strong growth of international trade and the increasing complexity of global supply chains are making a skilled work force essential for survival. Therefore, companies need effective recruitment strategies for logistics/SCM.

The survey respondents were asked to indicate what they thought were the most appealing aspects of logistics employment to present to potential recruits (figure 6.1). This revealed that many facets of a logistician's job are likely to have a positive impact on recruitment. Moreover, survey participants from developing and developed regions broadly agreed on the ratings regarding relative importance.

Common aspects such as work satisfaction, pay/benefits and job security ranked high on the list, but a "transparent career path to senior management" was considered the key aspect to promote. This point was also frequently mentioned in the interviews, which reflects the fact that young recruits are increasingly demanding clearer guidance from employers on their future career path. The recognition of logistics as a profession coupled with a raising of profession standards will also strengthen its appeal to potential applicants.

Emphasizing the importance of logistics to the economy is also felt to be a good way of attracting more people into the logistics sector, in particular to blue-collar jobs. As mentioned in the trucking case study, the status of truck driving could be elevated by highlighting its major contribution to the economy and social well-being. This can help to overcome the relatively low rating assigned to "prestige" in the survey. More could also be done to stress the importance of

Figure 6.1 Key Aspects for Recruitment

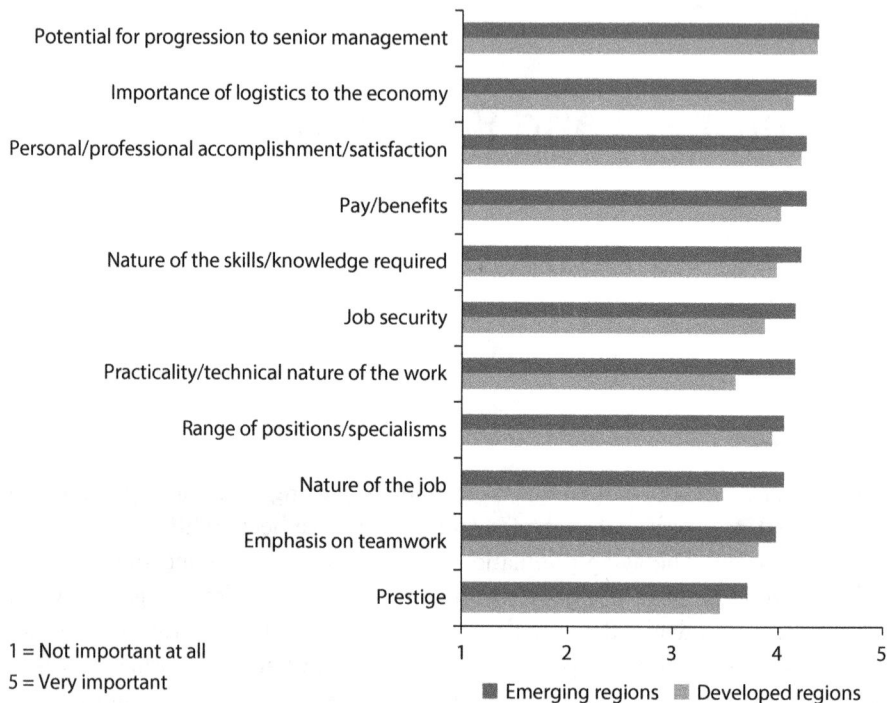

Potential for progression to senior management
Importance of logistics to the economy
Personal/professional accomplishment/satisfaction
Pay/benefits
Nature of the skills/knowledge required
Job security
Practicality/technical nature of the work
Range of positions/specialisms
Nature of the job
Emphasis on teamwork
Prestige

1 = Not important at all
5 = Very important

■ Emerging regions ▨ Developed regions

teamwork, job diversity and cross-functional perspectives in "selling" a career in logistics/SCM to the next generation of potential recruits.

"Employer branding" has also been advocated as a means of reinforcing recruitment. Cap Gemini et al. (2016) argue that "companies that invest as much time and resources into the employer brand as they do into their customer-facing brand create a competitive advantage when labor is scarce" (p. 39). The ability to recruit high caliber staff in a tight job market, such as that of logistics in many parts of the world, can become a competitive differentiator.

Recruitment channels: Interviewees from all regions broadly agreed on what the main recruitment channels for logistics positions should be. In fact, there were no differences between developing and developed countries on this issue. Online job platforms, advertisements in newspapers and magazines and social media are the most-used recruitment channels for white-collar jobs. The online channel is now an established, easy-to-access medium even in less developed countries. In addition, to these marketing instruments, referrals and word-of-mouth offer a valuable means of reaching out to potential employees. In developing countries where blue-collar workers are recruited locally from the surrounding communities, personal recommendations are crucial.

For top management positions, headhunting agencies are usually the first choice. In the past, potential recruits were usually headhunted from direct competitors. Due to the ongoing talent shortage in logistics, nowadays it has become common practice to lure logistics staff away from manufacturing and retail companies.

An efficient strategy for filling managerial entry-level positions is to recruit university students right after graduation. Logistics companies can establish initial connections with potential candidates even before graduation through guest lectures, internships or support with thesis projects. More proactive companies are identifying universities whose curricula and student intake match their logistics employment requirements.

Retention

The interviewees and survey respondents considered staff retention to be a key HR issue in logistics. Retention challenges are closely related to recruitment challenges: retaining employees in the company can be as important and as difficult as finding them in the open market. Consequently, many recruitment strategies also contribute to retaining people in the logistics sector as a whole and within specific firms. Providing high-caliber employees and promising candidates with clear career paths supports recruitment and retention simultaneously. The same holds true for pay, benefits and job security.

The online survey data presented in figure 6.2 show that retention of staff at the managerial level is a serious challenge in developing countries. The employees at this level are the ones who drive the adoption and implementation of new supply chain concepts, technologies and practices. The loss of key managers to other functions or sectors can have a debilitating effect on the development of logistics in developing markets. Companies in developed regions appear to fare much better in the retention of logistics managers.

These survey results must be qualified, however, as the majority of respondents from developed regions work for multi-national 3PLs. These businesses have competitive advantages over smaller players in the retention of senior managers, since they typically offer higher salaries, smoother career progression and

Figure 6.2 Employee Retention Ability

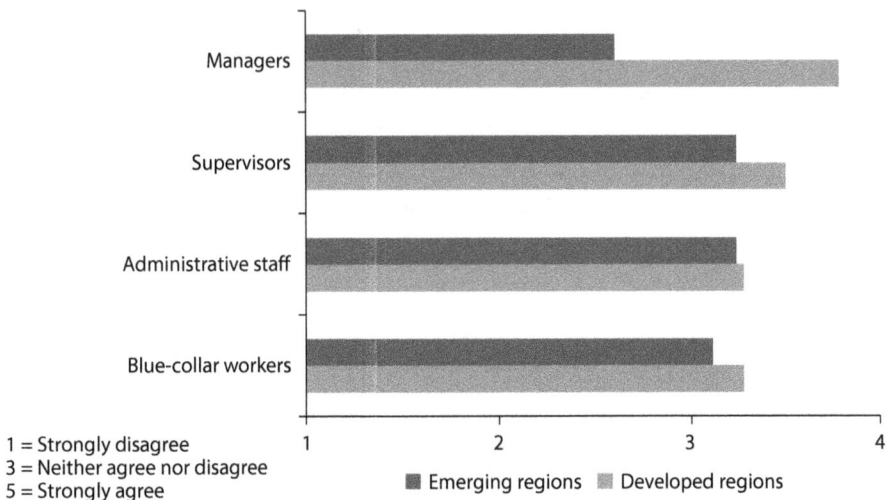

1 = Strongly disagree
3 = Neither agree nor disagree
5 = Strongly agree

■ Emerging regions ▨ Developed regions

Logistics Competencies, Skills, and Training • http://dx.doi.org/10.1596/978-1-4648-1140-1

access to an international working environment. Nevertheless, the interviewees argued that companies in the logistics sector should benchmark their salary levels to the market annually, to ensure that they are paying fair, competitive salaries. The retention of employees at lower tiers in the logistics job hierarchy appears to be less of an issue and of similar importance in developed and emerging (developing) markets.

Based on the interviews, the following guidelines for employee retention were derived:

Given their relatively slim profit margins and fierce competition, it is challenging for many 3PLs to compete on salary levels with other sectors such as manufacturing, marketing and finance. Therefore, interviewees suggested that 3PLs must apply retention strategies that also emphasize factors other than salary. This could be in the form of providing a clear, transparent career path for high-potential workers—at all levels. Blue-collar workers should be made aware of the opportunity to become a supervisor or shift supervisor in the future, meaning higher salary and greater responsibility. Administrative staff should be able to advance to office manager within the company, and junior managers to senior management.

Clearer logistics career paths need to be established and publicized. The Professional Development Stairway developed by Skills for Logistics in the United Kingdom illustrates a potential 10-step career path for workers in this sector, ascending from being unskilled new recruit to a logistics director (Skills for Logistics 2015) (figure 6.3). New entrants to the sector can, of course, join

Figure 6.3 Professional Development Stairway

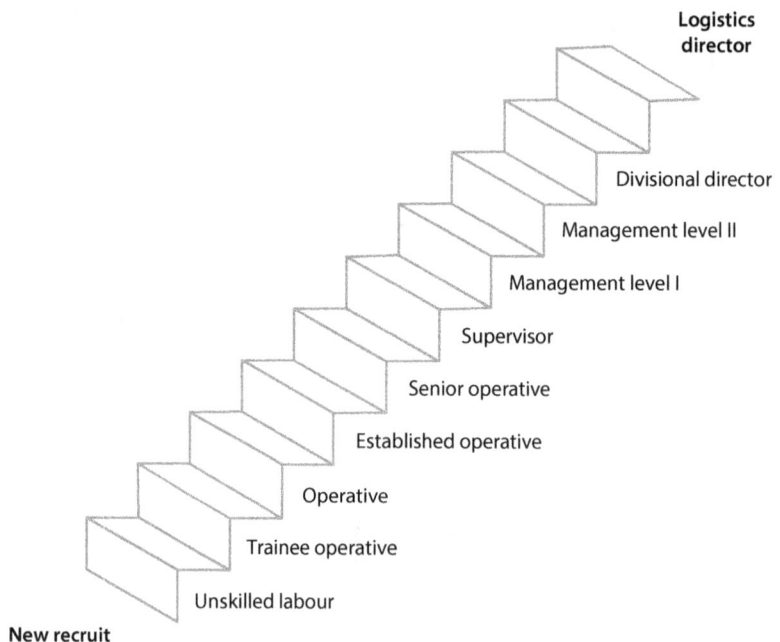

Source: Skills for Logistics 2015.

at any level and achieve differing levels of promotion during their careers. The stairway merely attempts to show at an industry-level the steps that an aspiring logistics employee might take. It differs from the hierarchy adopted by the present study not only in the number of grades but also in the exclusion of lower-level administrative roles.

A 2013 survey by Skills for Logistics in the United Kingdom indicated that staff retention was not a major issue, since staff turnover in logistics and SCM was rated, low, very low or non-existent (84 percent and 85 percent respectively) by a large sample of companies. The same survey also assessed the relative importance of a range of staff retention factors (table 6.1). The research suggests that the relatively low staff turnover rate in the United Kingdom may be partly due to companies effectively structuring their retention policies around this ranking of factors.

Two reasons for the relative unattractiveness of many logistics jobs is that the work environment is unpleasant and the work is often physically demanding. In order to make these jobs more appealing and comfortable for workers, employers can create better working conditions and invest in more materials handling equipment. Potential actions could include installing air conditioning systems in warehouses in tropical or sub-tropical regions, providing break-out areas, opening a canteen, planning more frequent breaks, etc. The additional cost of such upgrades must be balanced against the productivity benefits that accrue from having a stable, contented and well-motivated workforce.

Having the opportunity to grow and learn can be a tremendous motivator to stay in a company. Hand-in-hand with a transparent career path, investment in training and mentoring programs can yield healthy returns in the form of improved staff retention.

Easy but efficient ways of improving employee satisfaction and employer branding include celebrating the achievement of high performers, creating a great team atmosphere and company culture and acknowledging loyalty. For instance, firms can establish an "employee of the month" award in each warehouse, give small presents at anniversaries and organize annual company outings.

Table 6.1 Staff Retention Factors

Staff retention factors	Supply chain (%)	Logistics sector (%)
Terms and conditions (incl. pay and working hours)	45	34
Working environment	20	18
Limited opportunities elsewhere	19	17
Job satisfaction	18	23
How staff are treated (incl. receive recognition/are valued)	15	17
Job security	14	14
Company reputation	13	11
Training opportunities	9	6
Family-run business (incl. family members as staff)	5	7
Staff loyalty	5	9
Others	16	42

Source: Skills for Logistics 2014b.

These actions take limited effort to implement but often have a great impact. Supervisors and managers should be sensitive to employees' concerns.

Team-based incentives are a smart way of fostering close teamwork and bonding. If employees feel connected, they are less likely to switch employers, since they will not want to abandon their team. Furthermore, team-based incentives increase overall performance and productivity. Of course much of this is simply good management practice, applicable across all functions and sectors and not limited to logistics/SCM.

References

Cap Gemini, PennState Smeal College of Business, Penske, and Korn Ferry. 2016. "Third-Party Logistics Study: The State of Logistics Outsourcing." www.3plstudy.com.

Skills for Logistics. 2014b. *Industry Skills Survey: Supply Chain.* http://www.skillsforlogistics.org/media/24803/supply-chain-2014.docx, (accessed October 13, 2015).

———. 2015. *The Professional Development Stairway.* http://www.skillsforlogistics.org/products-services/the-professional-development-stairway/, (accessed October 11, 2015).

CHAPTER 7

The Role of the Public Sector in Enhancing Logistics Competence

Many of the specialists consulted during the study agreed that governments can play a useful role in the upgrading of logistics skills. Education and labor force planning are core functions of government, while logistics is central to economic development and social welfare, so it should not be difficult to justify government involvement in efforts to raise skill levels in the logistics sector. For governments aiming to improve their countries' logistics prospects, the case for supporting these efforts is particularly strong. Government support can take various forms.

Facilitator and Regulator

Facilitation of multi-stakeholder collaboration: It is generally acknowledged that solving the logistics skills problem will require the coordinated effort of numerous organizations, including businesses that provide and use logistics services, professional institutes, industry associations, training providers and labor unions. In some countries with mature logistics markets, collaborative initiatives can be industry-led. Often, however, governments must act as catalysts, bringing interested parties together and providing incentives for them to work on joint skill development strategies. In the United Kingdom, for example, the national government established a sector skills council specifically for logistics (called Skills for Logistics) comprising representatives of companies, labor unions and professional bodies India's government facilitated the National Skills Development Corporation (NSDC). It is a public-private partnership that aims to promote skill development by catalyzing the creation of large, high quality, for-profit vocational institutions. The NSDC has a dedicated logistics sector skills council.

Governments in Singapore, Dubai and Saudi Arabia have all organized professional logistics conferences on training, certification and recruitment that assembled all the main stakeholders. Organizing events like these is a relatively inexpensive way to facilitate fruitful collaboration. Government-sponsored multi-stakeholder collaborative initiatives can take various forms. They can, for example, commission research into the changing nature of logistics skill requirements, provide guidance to training providers, and run advisory programs for logistics businesses.

Setting and harmonization of competence standards: In countries with more mature logistics markets, professional institutes have played a lead role in defining and classifying logistics competencies and linking them to different levels of training. This systematic approach makes the skill development process much easier to manage and ensures the industry-wide recognition of qualifications. In countries with less-developed logistics markets in which professional institutes have little or no presence, governments may need to intervene to work with business in the setting of competence standards.

Rather than attempting to develop indigenous standards from scratch, it is usually preferable for governments to invite one of the major international logistics/SCM professional bodies (CILT, CSCMP or BVL) to introduce their standards, normally by establishing a local branch or chapter. For example, in association with the Chinese Communication and Transport Association, the Chinese government worked with CILT to promote the adoption of its certification programs in China. Under the standardization heading, governments can also promote the harmonization of certification schemes. The schemes used by major professional bodies and smaller nationally-based organizations are not fully aligned and would benefit from greater harmonization.

Regulatory policy: At one extreme, governments could legislate to force logistics companies to give employees a certain number of training hours per year. In most countries, a policy like this would be considered too interventionist, too dictatorial and not justified by the severity of the problem. There are very few examples of governments using regulatory controls to upgrade skill levels in any field, let alone logistics. As discussed above, governments can get involved in setting competence standards for staff working in particular fields, but this is different from imposing regulations. Survey respondents identified ways in which the relaxation of regulations could support logistics skill development. For example, in some countries quotas on the number of visas allocated to particular companies can restrict the number of logistics trainers admitted, inhibiting the international transfer of logistics know-how and skills.

Regulatory policies designed to improve safety and outlaw exploitative business practices can also indirectly make employment in the logistics sector more attractive, or at least less unattractive. For example, tightening and more effectively enforcing the restrictions and regulations on speeding, drivers' hours, vehicle overloading and maintenance standards can make the working environment safer and less stressful for truck drivers. For example, the Australian government has issued a "chain of responsibility" regulation as part of its national heavy vehicle regulator (NHVR) initiative. This applies to speeding, driver fatigue, vehicle mass, loading and dimensions.

The NHVR recognizes that apparently unlawful behavior by truck drivers is often influenced/controlled by the actions of other parties. Transport laws have often focused on the actions of drivers while failing to sufficiently recognize and regulate the behavior of carrier management and shippers. Chain of responsibility laws seek to guarantee that these other parties cannot encourage or compel drivers to undertake unlawful actions. These other parties are now legally liable for breaches of the Heavy Vehicle National Law (National Heavy Vehicle Regulator 2015).

Raising awareness about the crucial role of logistics skills and training: Government departments and agencies can be a useful source of information and promotional activity in the field of logistics. They already perform this role in many countries with regard to topics such as safety, energy efficiency and environmental sustainability. They could extend the range of advice they offer to logistics businesses to include training and skills development. This could be done in collaboration with industry associations and professional institutes. State-sponsored "logistics observatories" are being established in several emerging markets, particularly in Latin America. They can become an effective conduit for channeling information and advice on skills development to the industry in their countries. They can also act as repositories for much of the data required by the people delivering industrial training and higher-level courses at colleges and universities.

Where a logistics observatory is acting as a clearing house for information about international trends, innovations and best practice, it can support the global diffusion of logistics know-how. It is understood that a new logistics observatory being established in Morocco will gather information on human resource issues. Interconnecting national logistics observatories can facilitate the dissemination of information about logistics skills and training. For example, the Inter-American Development Bank is establishing a logistics observatory for Latin America which will interface the national observatories being set up in countries such as Chile and Mexico.

Education policy/curriculum development: Most governments exert an influence on the curricula taught in schools and, in some cases, institutions of higher education. They can encourage educational establishments to make more reference to logistics in their curricula, particularly at the secondary school level. This can take various forms: for example, logistics projects and case studies can be incorporated into the lesson plans of disciplines such as math, economics, business studies and geography. Education ministries can encourage schools, colleges and universities to include industrial field excursions in their curricula. They can include logistics facilities such as air freight hubs, ports and automated high-rack warehouses, exposing students to logistics infrastructure and operations that they would otherwise never see. This can raise the status and prestige of the logistics sector in the eyes of the younger generation. The main goal is to raise the level of awareness of logistics as a possible career choice and show how the technical knowledge acquired in core subjects can find practical applications in logistics.

Direct Support and Intervention

Financial support for training initiatives:

(a) *Direct:* This involves investment in government-controlled training programs. A government can either run them itself or outsource them to specialized agencies. The UK government's SAFED program, which to date has trained around 10,000 truck and van drivers in "safe and fuel efficient driving techniques," is an example of direct financial support. In this type of initiative, government assumes a "hands-on" role in building logistics training capability. Another example is the Thai Industrial Ministry, which subsidizes training sessions held by certified training agencies (e.g., APICS trainers). Employers that send their logistics employees to these training sessions can be reimbursed for 50 percent of the accumulated expenses.

(b) *Indirect:* With this type of support, governments incentivize other organizations to increase the level of logistics skill/competence. This raises several issues:

(i) Which organizations should be eligible? A narrow definition of logistics would confine financial support to organizations whose main activity is freight transport, warehousing, materials handling, etc., although this would exclude the producers, wholesalers and retailers that undertake logistical tasks on an in-house and ancillary basis. Seedcorn funding can be made available for start-up enterprises to encourage existing educational/training organizations to diversify into logistics/SCM or to promote collaborative initiatives involving several stakeholders. Financial support can also be channeled through training providers such as colleges or professional institutes, as is currently happening in the United States as part of the US Department of Labor's LINCS (Leveraging, Integrating, Networking, Coordinating Supplies) Program for supply chain management education and certification (Blasgen 2015). A consortium of 9 colleges and 3 universities is administering this $24.5 million program.

The South African Ministry of Labor established the Transport Education and Training Authority (TETA), which is responsible for education, training and skills development in the transport sector. TETA is part of the country-wide Skills Education Training Authorities (SETA) Initiative. Companies pay a small premium on salary taxes for education and training. If they send their employees to TETA/SETA training courses, they can receive reimbursements for the extra tax payments. These employers are financially incentivized to train their workforces. This could be one of the factors explaining why South Africa's LPI Logistics Competence score outperforms its GDP per capita.

(ii) What type of financial support should be provided? A standard range of fiscal incentives could be deployed, including:

- Per capita allowance for each person receiving training, possibly graduated by skill level
- Tax rebates for corporate expenditure on training/skills development
- Block grants for setting up training units/businesses

(iii) How can governments ensure that the money is used appropriately? In countries where corruption is rife, there is a danger that much of the money allocated for logistics training will be misappropriated. The risk of this happening in the logistics sector is probably greater than in others because of the relatively high levels of illegality in the trucking industry. There can be tighter monitoring of training programs in which the public funds are paid to training providers and where it is linked to an institutionally-recognized examination and certification system.

Raising skill levels in state-owned logistics businesses: Governments have a major stake in logistics businesses around the world. Many rail freight companies, postal systems and port authorities are state-owned, often giving governments a significant influence over the way they are managed. These nationalized logistics enterprises can be used to set a good example in training and skills development to other private companies. Since they collectively employ a large proportion of a country's total logistics workforce, they can also play a key role in building a national training capability and become a source of skilled labor for other sectors of the logistics market.

Using public procurement to gain leverage on logistics skill levels: Governments are major buyers of transport and logistics services, handing them some influence over businesses tendering for this work. Levels of skill development and staff training could be included as a selection criterion in the award of contracts to logistics providers. This would not only incentivize these providers to invest more in training; it should also improve the quality and efficiency of the outsourced services.

Supplementing infrastructure development with investment in human capital: It has become quite common for investment in transport infrastructure to be accompanied by funds for capacity building, particularly when the funding comes from international organizations such as the World Bank. Capacity building often includes financial support for training/skills development in the design, management and operation of the new infrastructure. Its scope could be broadened to include upskilling the logistics/SCM workforce to ensure that businesses make effective use of the new transport infrastructure. For example, the Indonesian Port Authority is currently undertaking a major port investment program and to support this initiative, has enrolled a large group of its senior managers in an Executive MBA program with a strong logistics focus in the Kühne Logistics University.

Attaching greater weight to labor availability on spatial planning: Our study has highlighted the geographical dimension to logistics labor shortages at both regional and urban levels. Agencies responsible for land-use planning at these various levels could play a role in prioritizing labor availability as a locational criterion when granting planning permission for logistics-related development. The actual mix of public policy initiatives and the emphasis they are given will reflect socio-economic conditions and political preferences within the country. In terms of a public policy response to the logistics skills shortage, there is no "one-size-fits-all" proposal.

Implementing the initiatives listed above can also involve several government ministries. Logistics typically falls into a gap between the responsibilities of different ministries, such as transport, trade and industry, while logistics training should be a concern of the ministry of education. Getting all these ministries to make a coordinated response to the logistics skills shortage can be difficult.

Governments addressing this issue for the first time can also benefit from the experience of countries with more mature logistics markets which already have advanced training and certification programs in place. They could also benefit from forming partnerships/alliances with other neighboring governments that are themselves at an early stage of developing their logistics competence and logistics training capability. Organizations such as the World Bank and the UN support the formation of multi-national partnerships and have demonstrated their effectiveness in fields such transport and urban development. The World Bank also operates an *e-communities* website for the exchange of advice and good practice between countries in a range of fields, including transport. This online forum could be used to stimulate interest in logistics skills/training initiatives and share experiences among national governments.

References

Blasgen, R. 2015. "Announcing the Next Generation of Supply Chain Career Programs." *CSCMP's Supply Chain Quarterly* 2.

National Heavy Vehicle Regulator. 2015. *Safety, Accreditation & Compliance.* https://www.nhvr.gov.au/safety-accreditation-compliance/chain-of-responsibility, (accessed September 15, 2015).

CHAPTER 8

Logistics Competence Maturity Matrix

During the course of this study it became obvious that countries differ substantially in their logistics competence maturity. These differences are multi-dimensional. Developing and developed countries differ in the level of logistics competence, the availability of skilled labor at all occupational levels, access to educational institutions specializing in logistics, company involvement in training and development programs, and the ability to retain highly-skilled employees. In order to give governments more specific guidance, a logistics competence maturity matrix was constructed on the basis of the survey results, interviews, as well as literature and focus group discussions. This matrix classifies countries in terms of current levels of logistics competence and recommends an appropriate list of action points. Assessment of their current logistics competence levels is based on the logistics quality and competence scores presented in the 2014 LPI report. On a scale of 1.00–5.00, three maturity classes were differentiated:

- Basic logistics competence maturity (competence score: 1.00–2.74)
- Intermediate logistics competence maturity (2.75–3.33)
- Advanced logistics competence maturity (3.34–5.00)

Figure 8.1 summarizes the general recommendations for logistics competence development in these three categories of countries. It lists action points for each of the four main stakeholder groups: government, companies, as well as educational institutions and logistics associations. Many of these points apply to all four levels in the employment hierarchy.

As general advice, this report encourages countries to learn from the experience of those at higher maturity levels. The process of identifying national role models should take account of economic development (in terms of GDP per capita), population size, economic structure, key industries, geography, climate and infrastructure.

Figure 8.1 Logistics Competence Maturity Matrix

Stakeholder Guideline for Logistics Competence Development
Based on LPI 2014 "Logistics Quality & Competence" Score

Country logistics competence maturity (Scale: 1 to 5)	Basic (1.00–2.74)	Intermediate (2.75–3.33)	Advanced (3.34–5.00)
Sample countries	Belarus, Uruguay, Kenya, Somalia	Greece, Chile, Brazil, Indonesia, Egypt	Germany, Singapore, United States, China
Recommended stakeholder actions	**Governments:** • Invest in basic school education (regardless of logistics) • Supplement infrastructure investments with logistics capability investment • Issue laws & regulations that support logistics competence development • Facilitate multi-stakeholder collaboration • Encourage and advice to promote logistics **Companies:** • Implement regular in-house training on all hierarchical levels by internal experts **Educational institutions:** • Offer logistics courses & degrees • Collaborate with developed institutions abroad • Leverage logistics associations and public-private-partnerships **Logistics associations:** • Offer training at discounted rates • Consult governments	**Governments:** • Provide direct and indirect support for training initiatives • Raise skills levels in state-owed logistics business • Support knowledge transfer from mature regions with laws & regulations **Companies:** • Design standardized training programs with external input (associations and training agencies) **Educational institutions:** • Facilitate collaboration with local companies and international universities • Design up-to-date logistics curriculum and adapt teaching styles • Design logistics student exchange programs **Logistics associations:** • Setup branch offices • Provide train-the-trainer education • Organize frequent trainings for all levels of certification	**Governments:** • Consider additional funding for world-class logistics education **Companies:** • Consider further development of soft and leadership skills since logistics skills knowledge is already advanced **Educational institutions:** • Set-up joint-logistics and SCM programs with universities abroad (double degrees) • Consider branch campuses in emerging countries to support logistics education • Keep curricula updated to reflect the latest trends and innovations **Logistics associations:** • Collaborate closely with industry to keep training curricula up-to-date

In this respect, it is interesting to compare the provision of logistics training in country that is aspiring to become a logistics hub with one which has already gained this status. Jamaica is planning to be a major logistics center for the Caribbean, but recognizes that to achieve this status the country will have to raise its level of logistics expertise, partly building on the logistics training currently offered by the University of the Caribbean and the Caribbean Maritime institute. In contrast, in the UAE there around 90 logistics courses, ranging from short (40 hour) diploma courses to graduate degrees are offered by a variety of academic and professional institutes including local branches of some US and European universities. This high level of training provision is consistent with the UAE's status as a well-established global logistics hub.

The recommendations in the matrix are cumulative and incremental. Obviously, intermediate countries should follow recommendations for basic countries, but advanced countries should not overlook suggestions for countries at the basic and intermediate levels.

Logistics Competence Maturity Self-Assessment Tool

A questionnaire-based tool has been devised to allow countries to assess the maturity of their logistics market in terms of skills and training. This is intended to provide only a rough guide to a country's maturity and involves a significant amount of subjective judgment. Respondents have to answer fifteen questions classified into three categories relating to the educational system, logistics competencies and the provision of training (appendix D).

They indicate their level of agreement or disagreement with fifteen statements using a 5-point Likert-scale. The cells can be selected and the corresponding number of points entered in the circles on the right. After completion, the numbers of points in the circles are summed to give an overall numerical index. Depending on where this index falls within the numerical ranges at the bottom of the table, a country's maturity level can be rated as advanced, intermediate or basic. This maturity rating can be related to the guidance offered to the various stakeholder groups within the country by consulting the matrix in figure 8.1.

CHAPTER 9

Conclusion

The main aim of this study has been to assess the extent to which logistics competencies, skills, and training are currently lacking and to analyze the nature of this deficiency. The study has attempted to diagnose the main causes of the logistics skills shortage and, hence, this market failure. They include: low salary levels compared to other sectors, relatively poor working conditions (particularly in low and middle income countries), the low prestige and status of logistics occupations in many cultures and societies, the demographic structure of the logistics work-force in developed countries, the limited supply of labor in remote areas where logistics hubs are frequently located, a lack of vocational school preparation for logistics careers various cultural constraints and the increasing technical complexity of the logistics function.

The report highlights the need for a major expansion in logistics training and skills development. Developing regions are lagging behind developed countries in terms of training budgets and capability, the range and quality of training provision and the adoption of professional standards. Often, training is limited to short-term, on-the-job induction provided by colleagues during daily operations.

Alleviating the logistics skill problem will demand a multi-stakeholder approach. The report describes the roles of the various stakeholder groups involved in the training, assessment, certification, recruitment and retention of logistics staff. These stakeholders, including companies, logistics associations, higher educational institutes, external training agencies and governments, have a mutual interest in this effort. The report suggests different ways in which working individually and in collaboration, these stakeholders can tackle labor shortages and facilitate the upskilling of logistics labor through training and development.

The report has identified a range of best practices in the promotion of competence development that are particularly relevant for developing markets. Training initiatives are proposed that could be implemented even on tight budgets and in places where the educational system and logistics sector are at a relatively low level of maturity. They include multiple stakeholder collaboration in the provision of dual education and apprenticeships, experiential and blended learning approaches and the updating of college curricula on logistics and SCM.

As for recruitment and retention strategies: The advantages of a career in logistics (internationality, working in inter-cultural teams, stimulating working environment, mobility, key contribution to the economy and general wellbeing, involvement in technological innovation, etc.) need to be underlined more strongly. In some countries and sectors of the logistics market, the pay and conditions will need to be improved to attract a sufficient number of high-caliber recruits. As far as recruitment and retention are concerned, the prescriptions are similar for countries of all income levels. They are also very similar to those for other business activities (e.g., transparent career paths, appealing working environments, investment in the development of the workforce and building a greater sense of belonging to the team and company) and represent what is considered good management practice today. The concept of employer branding also needs to be grasped by firms in the logistics sector.

The study examines the possible role of government in helping to close the logistics competence gap. There are eleven ways in which governments can try to enhance competence levels across their countries' logistics workforce:

- Facilitate multiple stakeholder collaboration
- Set and harmonize competence standards
- Use regulatory policy both directly and indirectly
- Raising awareness about the crucial role of logistics skills and training
- Prioritize logistics in education policy and/or curriculum development
- Provide financial support for training initiatives
- Raise skill levels in state-owned logistics enterprises
- Using public procurement to gain leverage on logistics skill levels
- Supplement infrastructure development with investment in human capital
- Attaching greater weight to labor availability in spatial planning.

Finally, the report presents a logistics competence maturity matrix that classifies countries into three categories in terms of their 2014 LPI competence index (basic, intermediate and advanced). A simple questionnaire can be used to differentiate countries into these three maturity levels (see appendix D). The matrix provides guidance on how countries at each level can upgrade their logistics skill levels. Advice is given for each of the stakeholder groups in a country, assuming that they will be working together to address what is unquestionably one of the major challenges currently facing the logistics industry worldwide. In the longer term, increased mechanization and automation may reduce the labor intensity of the logistics sector providing a technological response to this HR challenge. For the foreseeable future, however, it will have to be addressed by more conventional means.

Selected Literature Related to Logistics Skills, Competence, and Training

Author	Title	Publisher	Country published	Year published
Alliance of Sectors Skills Council, Scotland (Alliance Scotland)	Freight Logistics and Warehousing Industry: Scottish Sector Profile 2011	UK Sector Skills Councils (SSCs) Scotland	Scotland	2011
APICS 2009 Future Leaders	APICS Supply Chain Manager Competency Model	APICS The Association for Operations Management	United States	2011
Bodegraven, Art Van; Ackerman, Kenneth B.	Mastering the skills required for Today's "New Basics" of Supply Chain Management	Supply Chain 247	United States	2013
Bölsche, Dorit; Klumpp, Matthias; Abidi, Hella	Specific Competencies in Humanitarian Logistics Education	Journal of Humanitarian Logistics and Supply Chain Management. Vol. 3, No. 2	Germany	2013
Chaudhuri, Abhijit; Bindlish, Rishabh; Rao CV, Narayan; Deshpande, Prasad; Deshpande, Dayanand	Skills Set Challenges for the Pharma Supply Chain	Supply Chain Management Professional. Vol. 1, No. 6	India	2013
Dazmin, Daud	Logistics Educational Needs of Malaysia: A Conceptual Study	Academic Research International, Vol. 3, No. 3	Malaysia	2012
Dittmann, J. Paul	Skills and Competencies that Supply Chain Managers will need	Supply Chain Management Review	United States	2012
Ellinger, Alexander; Ellinger, Andrea D.	Leveraging human resource development expertise to improve supply chain managers' skills and competencies	European Journal of Training and Development. Vol. 38, No. 1/2, Pg. 118–135	United States	2014

table continues next page

Author	Title	Publisher	Country published	Year published
Ellinger, Alexander; Ellinger, Andrea D.; Keller, Scott B.	Logistics Managers' Learning Environment and Firm Performance	Journal of Business Logistics. Vol. 23, No. 1	United States	2002
Gammelgaard, Britta Larson, Paul D.	Logistics skills and competencies for supply chain management	Journal of Business Logistics. Vol. 22, No. 2, Pg. 27–50	United States	2001
Goffnett, Sean P.; Cook, Robert L.; Williams Zachary; Gibson, Brian J.	Understanding satisfaction with Supply Chain Management Careers: An exploratory Study	The International Journal of Logistics Management. Vol. 23, No. 1, Pg. 135–158	United States	2012
Gravier, Michael J.; Farris, M. Theodore	An analysis of logistics pedagogical literature: Past and future trends in curriculum, content, and pedagogy	The International Journal of Logistics Management. Vol. 19, No. 2, Pg. 233–253	United States	2008
Handfield, Robert B.	Key Trends, Skills, and Knowledge Required for the Supply Chain Manager of the Future	Supply Chain Redesign	United States	2011
Handfield, Robert; Straube, Frank; Pfohl, Hans-Christian; Wieland, Andreas	Trends and Strategies in Logistics and Supply Chain Management: Embracing Global Logistics Complexity to drive Market Advantage	DVV Media Group GmbH	Germany	2013
Heyns, Gert; Carstens, Stephen	The Skills set required for Supply Chain Management in Southern Africa	Carpathian Logistics Congress (CLC)	South Africa	2012
Heyns, Gert; Rose, Luke	Skills required in the Supply Chain Industry in South Africa	Journal of Transport and Supply Chain Management	South Africa	2012
Hoberg, Kai; Flöthmann, Christoph	Experiential Learning for Humanitarian Logistics, in: Humanitarian Logistics in Asia-Pacific.	Kühne Foundation Book Series on Logistics 19. Haupt Publisher	Germany	2012
Hohenstein, Nils-Ole; Feisel, Edda; Hartmann, Evi	Human Resources Management Issues in Supply Chain Management Research: A systematic Literature Review from 1998 to 2014	International Journal of Physical Distribution and Logistics Management. Vol. 44, No. 6, Pg. 434–463	Germany	2014
Hsieh, Li-Yang; Lu, Yang-Jui; Lin, Hsiang-Sheng; Lee, Yao-Hsien	With Blended Learning Information Operational System Design in Response to Globalized Logistics Talent Training	The 2nd International Workshop on Learning Technology for Education in Cloud. Pg. 61–71	Netherlands, Taiwan, China	2014
Hung Lau, Kwok; Gu, Meihua	Section 9—Service Supply Chains and Emerging Markets: "From Cheap Labor to Logistics Competency: The Next Move for China?"	School of Business IT and Logistics	Australia	2012
ICRA Managing Consulting Services Limited	Human Resource and Skill Requirements in the Transportation, Logistics, Warehousing and Packaging Sector	National Skill Development Corporation (NSDC)	India	2009

table continues next page

Author	Title	Publisher	Country published	Year published
Kam, Booi H.; Chan, Caroline; Paul, Bageswari Raju	Profiles of Postgraduate Supply Chain and Logistics Programs	School of Business IT and Logistics; College of Business	Australia	2012
Kisperska-Moron, Danuta	Changing Requirements for Managerial Skills and Competencies in Contemporary Supply Chains	University of Economics in Katowice	Poland	2010
Kisperska-Moron, Danuta	Evolution of Competencies of Logistics and Supply Chain Managers	Electronic Scientific Journal of Logistics. Vol. 6, Iss. 3, No. 3, Pg. 21–31	Poland	2010
Kovacs, G, Tatham, P. and Larson, P.D. (2012)	What skills are needed to be a humanitarian logistician?	Journal of Business Logistics, 33 (3), Pg. 245–258.	United States	2012
Lim, Yu Pei; Dazmin Daud; Kholyn Ruran, Jonathan	Perceptions of logistics students on internship program: the case of private higher institution in Malaysia	Canadian Social Science. Vol. 8, No. 4, Pg. 1–7	Canada	2012
Murphy, Paul; Poist, Richard F.	Skills Requirements of Senior-Level Logisticians: A Longitudinal Assessment	Supply Chain Management: An International Journal, Vol. 12, No. 6, Pg .423–431	United States	2007
Murphy, Paul; Poist, Richard F.	Skill Requirements of Contemporary Senior- and Entry-Level Logistics Managers: A Comparative Analysis	Transportation Journal. Vol. 45, No. 3, Pg. 46–60	United States	2006
Niine, Tarvo; Lend, Enno	Logistics Management versus Supply Chain Management—the Crystallization of Debate for Academic and Practical Clarity	Logistics and Sustainable Transport, Vol. 4, No. 1	Estonia	2013
Ozment, John; Keller, Scott B.	The Future of Logistics Education	Transportation Journal. Vol. 50, No. 1, Pg. 65–83	United States	2011
Pahim, K.M.; Jemali, H.S.; Mohamad, S.J.A.N.S.	A conceptual paper for human capital in the logistics industry in Malaysia	Business, Engineering and Industrial Applications (ISBEIA). Pg. 357–362	Malaysia	2011
Porasmaa, Minna; Kotonen, Ulla	Development of Logistics Thinking and the Requirements It Sets on Logistics Skills and Competences	Faculty of Business Studies	Finland	2011
Ruske, Klaus-Dieter; Kauschke, Peter; Von der Gracht, Heiko	Global Transportation and Logistics 2030—Volume 5: Winning the Talent Race	PricewaterhouseCoopers International Limited (PwCIL)	Germany	2012
Southwest Skills for Life Unit	Southwest Skills for Life Briefing in the Logistics Sector	Skills for Logistics (SfL)	United Kingdom	2007
Thomas, Anisya; Mizushima, Mitsuko	Logistics Training: Necessity or Luxury?	Forced Migration Review (FRM). Vol. 22, Pg. 60–61	United States	2005
Trunick, Perry A.	Supply Chain Graduates: Now What?	Inbound Logistics Magazine. Pg. 78–82	United States	2011
Vokurka, Robert J.	Supply Chain Manager Competencies	SAM Advanced Management Journal. Vol. 76, No. 2 .Pg. 23–28	United States	2011

table continues next page

Author	Title	Publisher	Country published	Year published
Winters, Gwenn; Skelton, Adam; Begum, Shahima; Parkes, Shabana	Logistics Employer Skills Survey 2013	Skills for Logistics	United Kingdom	2014
Wu, Yen-Chu Jim	Contemporary Logistics Education: An international Perspective	International Journal of Physical Distribution and Logistics Management. Vol. 37, No.7, Pg. 504–528	Taiwan, China	2007
Wu, Yen-Chu Jim	Skills Requirements for Logistics Licensing in Taiwan, China	Supply Chain Management: An International Journal, Vol. 11, No. 5, Pg. 415–424	Taiwan, China	2006
Zhong, Xiao Jun; Li, Ping; Yin, Jie	Research on Cultivation Model for Logistics Talents of Universities in Ningbo: A Case Study of Zhejiang Wangli University	Advanced Materials Research. Vol. 734–737, Pg. 3356–3361	Switzerland	2013
Zhu, Minjie; Zhang, Jianwei; Bao, Shenghua	Research on the Cultivation of Logistics Engineering Application Talents By the Diversification School-enterprise Cooperation	Elsevier Ltd	China	2011

Example of Continuing Professional Development (CPD) for Logistics

SAMPLE CONTINUING PROFESSIONAL DEVELOPMENT (CPD) PLAN

It is The Chartered Institute of Logistics and Transport's policy that applications for Chartered Fellow, Chartered Member and Member are accompanied by a CPD Plan covering the forthcoming 2 years. This form is designed to help you summarise your CPD Plan, if you already have a CPD Plan of your own or e.g. a Career Development Plan, this may be submitted instead on the condition it meets our requirements.

Objectives – what do I want / need to learn?	Action – What will I do to achieve this?	What resources/support do I need	Measurement – What will my success criteria be?	Target dates for review/completion
Attain certificate of professional competence (CPC)	Attend a suitable training course for a practitioner	An approved centre such as CILT CILT Knowledge Centre access	Passing the course/ accreditation	October 2016
Keeping industry/ sector knowledge up-to-date	Read and Research	Technical Periodicals such as Logistics & Transport Focus Relevant web sites and CILT Knowledge Centre	Increased awareness and knowledge	Ongoing on a monthly basis
Increase knowledge of: the impact of E-commerce on the supply chain or, Transport regulations and legislation	Attend at least 4 CILT relevant events per year	Support required by employer in terms of time commitments	Increase in business levels and customer feedback due to increased knowledge and best practices	Ongoing – Review on annual basis to ensure events have been attended
To learn French	Private lessons/ College course	Will power	Using second language to converse with company clients	August 2016

Supplementary Survey Results

a. My organization provides high quality training courses

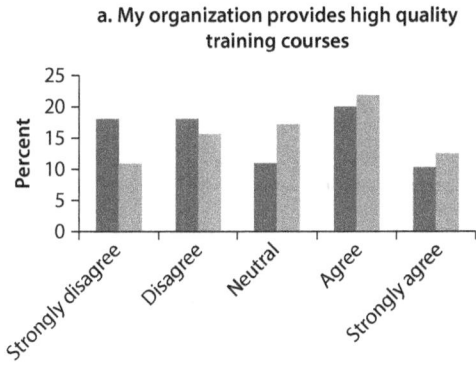

b. My organization provides regularly evaluates the training needs of their employees

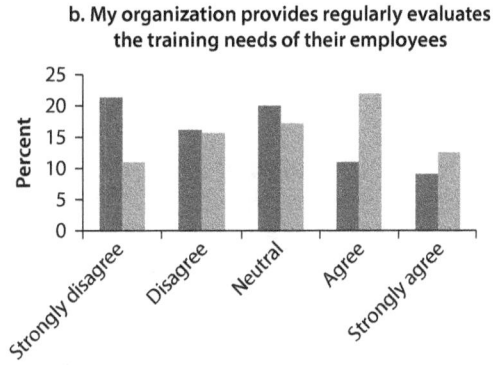

c. My organization provides a sufficient budget for training courses

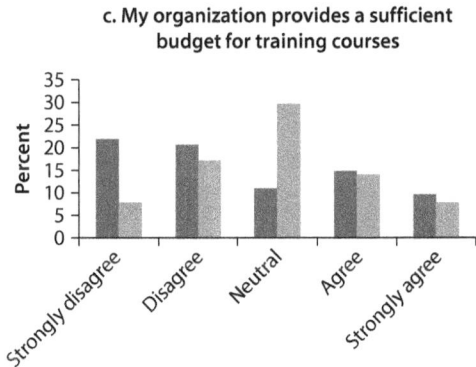

d. How is the turnover rate of your logistics talent in the past 12 months compared to the average in your organization?

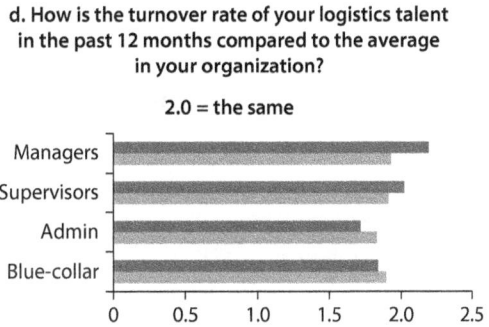

■ Emerging regions
■ Developed regions

figure continues next page

e. How effective are the employee development methods (if any) used by your organization?

1 = very ineffective
5 = very effective

■ Emerging regions
▨ Developed regions

Demographics

	Emerging regions				
	n	*%*		*n*	*%*
Region			**Industry**		
Sub-Saharan Africa	105	67.7	3PL (Transportation + Warehousing)	57	36.8
South-East Asia	23	14.8	Consulting/IT Service	22	14.2
Middle East / North Africa	17	11.0	Logistics association	21	13.5
Central Asia	9	5.8	Academia	18	11.6
Latin America	1	0.6	Transportation only	16	10.3
Total	**219**	**100%**	Manufacturing	9	5.8
			Retail/Wholesale	6	3.9
			Warehousing only	6	3.9
			Revenue (in Euro)		
Top 10 Countries (optional)			below 10mn	50	32.3
Zimbabwe	15	9.7	10–250mn	50	32.3
Nigeria	12	7.7	>250mn–1bn	24	15.5
Ghana	11	7.1	>1–10bn	10	6.5
Pakistan	11	7.1	above 10bn	14	9.0
Zambia	10	6.5			
Uganda	9	5.8	**Business experience (in years)**		
India	8	5.2	less than 2	12	7.7
Ethiopia	7	4.5	2–5	9	5.8
Sudan	4	2.6	>5–10	47	30.3
Tanzania	4	2.6	>10–25	68	43.9
			more than 25	19	12.3

table continues next page

Emerging Regions					
	n	%		n	%
Function			**Hierarchical level**		
Supply Chain Management	61	39.4	Board level	8	5.2
Logistics	50	32.3	Senior management	55	35.5
General management	14	9.0	Middle management	65	41.9
Procurement	10	6.5	Lower management	15	9.7
Human resources/ Training & development	7	4.5	Non-managerial role	7	4.5
Other	6	3.9	Other (please specify)	5	3.2
Production	2	1.3			
Marketing/Sales	2	1.3			
Controlling/Finance	2	1.3			
Quality	1	0.6			

Developed Regions					
	n	%		n	%
Region			**Industry**		
Europe	59	92.2	3PL (Transportation + Warehousing)	14	21.9
Australia / Oceania	4	6.3	Manufacturing	10	15.6
North America	1	1.6	Retail/Wholesale	9	14.1
Total	**64**	**100%**	Academia	9	14.1
			Logistics association	9	14.1
			Consulting/IT Service	7	10.9
Countries (optional)			Transportation only	6	9.4
Romania	11	17.2	Warehousing only	0	0.0
Greece	9	14.1			
Ukraine	9	14.1	**Revenue (in Euro)**		
Poland	7	10.9	below 10mn	19	29.7
Ireland {Republic}	2	3.1	10-250mn	22	34.4
Australia	1	1.6	>250mn-1bn	12	18.8
Belgium	1	1.6	>1-10bn	4	6.3
Benin	1	1.6	above 10bn	3	4.7
Germany	1	1.6			
Hungary	1	1.6	**Business experience (in years)**		
Malta	1	1.6	less than 2	1	1.6
New Zealand	1	1.6	2-5	3	4.7
Norway	1	1.6	>5-10	14	21.9
Russian Federation	1	1.6	>10-25	32	50.0
Slovenia	1	1.6	more than 25	14	21.9
United Kingdom	1	1.6			

table continues next page

Developed Regions					
	n	%		n	%
Function			**Hierarchical level**		
Logistics	22	34.4	Board level	11	17.2
General management	18	28.1	Senior management	26	40.6
Supply Chain Management	12	18.8	Middle management	6	9.4
Other	5	7.8	Lower management	18	28.1
Human resources / Training & development	4	6.3	Non-managerial role	3	4.7
Marketing/Sales	3	4.7	Other (please specify)	0	0.0
Other	0	0.0			

Self-Assessment Tool

The questionnaire can serve as a quick tool for assessing a country's logistics competence maturity.

Instruction: *Answer each question. After completion, make note of the points scored per question (strongly disagree = 1 point, strongly agree = 5) and calculate the sum of points. The numerical ranges shown at the bottom of the table will indicate the country's maturity level. The corresponding action points for various stakeholder groups can be found in Figure 24.*

	Points allocated					
	1	2	3	4	5	
	Strongly disagree	*Disagree*	*Neutral*	*Agree*	*Strongly agree*	*Points scored:*
Section 1: Logistics education						
Q1.1: Numerous educational institutions in my country (e.g., colleges, universities) offer programs specialized in logistics.						◯
Q1.2: Companies collaborate closely with universities and vocational schools in the development of logistics courses.						◯
Q1.3: Significant numbers of students take logistics courses in foreign universities and return to take up logistics management posts.						◯
Q1.4: Western educational institutions that offer logistics programs have established branch campuses in my country.						◯
Q1.5: Apprenticeships or dual education programs in logistics are common in my country.						◯
Section 2: Logistics competence						
Q2.1: Certification programs exist for logistics skills and competencies and are widely used.						◯

table continues next page

		Points allocated					
		1	2	3	4	5	Points scored:
		Strongly disagree	Disagree	Neutral	Agree	Strongly agree	
Q2.2:	Multi-national 3PLs have a substantial share of the national logistics market.						○
Q2.3:	There is a network of recruitment agencies specializing in the employment of logistic staff.						○
Q2.4:	Professional logistics associations have a strong presence in the country.						○
Q2.5:	A significant proportion of logistics managers have specialized qualifications in logistics.						○

Section 3: Company training & development

Q3.1:	Numerous private training providers offer logistics courses.						○
Q3.2:	It is common for logistics companies to invest in the training and professional development of their employees.						○
Q3.3:	The government provides support for the training of logistics employees.						○
Q3.4:	Logistics is recognized to be a major sector of the economy and an important source of employment.						○
Q3.5	There are well established career paths for logistics employees within the country.						○

Maturity level	Points
Advanced:	75–51
Intermediate:	50–31
Basic:	30–0

TOTAL [　　　]

Results from the World Bank Logistics Performance Index Survey 2015/2016

To supplement the World Bank/KLU report on logistics skills and training, the 2016 edition of the Logistics Performance Index survey for the first time included a question on logistics skills and competencies. Respondents were asked to indicate the availability (from "very high" to "very low") of qualified personnel for four groups of logistics personnel:

1. Operative staff, for example, truck drivers or warehouse pickers
2. Administrative staff, for example, traffic planners, expediters or warehouse clerks
3. Logistics supervisors, for example, warehouse shift leaders or traffic controllers
4. Logistics managers, for example, those responsible for transport, warehousing operations or supply chain management.

Results from the 2016 LPI survey bolster the World Bank/KLU report's findings that logistics faces a global shortage of qualified staff. Qualified staff is scarce to varying degrees at all four occupational levels in all countries, but particularly in the countries that form the bottom quintile in the LPI.[1] In those countries, the shortage of logistics staff in the "mid tiers," that is, administrative staff and supervisors, is most acute. A similar picture emerges in the second-lowest LPI quintile, where the share of low or very low availability was rated at around a third for all four occupational levels. The problem of skills shortages is less acute but equally present in the third, fourth and fifth LPI quintile.

When broken down by geographic region, Latin America and the Caribbean emerges as the region with the highest skills gap across all employee groups. A full 43 percent of respondents for instance indicated that the availability of logistics managers, that is, those with the most sophisticated responsibilities, was either "low" or "very low." Yet also for each of the three remaining employee

Figure E.1 Respondents Indicating "Low" or "Very Low" Availability of Qualified Personnel in the Respective Employee Groups, by LPI Quintile

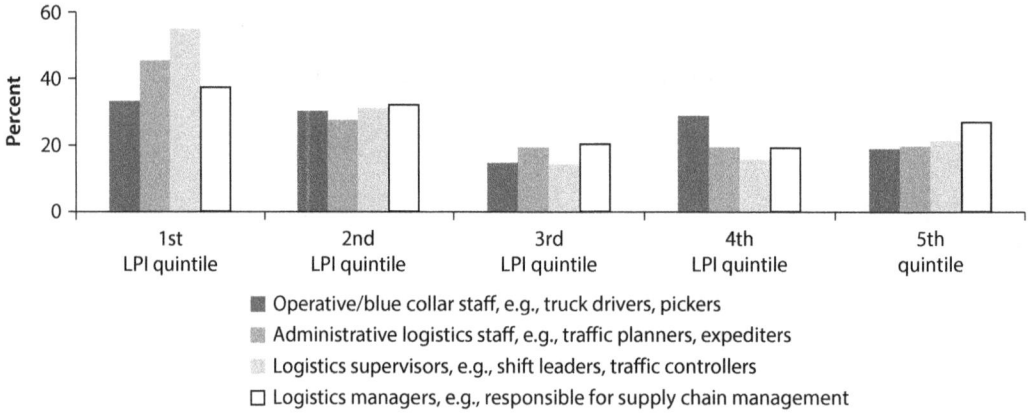

■ Operative/blue collar staff, e.g., truck drivers, pickers
▒ Administrative logistics staff, e.g., traffic planners, expediters
░ Logistics supervisors, e.g., shift leaders, traffic controllers
☐ Logistics managers, e.g., responsible for supply chain management

Source: Logistics Performance Index 2016.

Figure E.2 Respondents Indicating "Low" or "Very Low" Availability of Qualified Personnel in the Respective Employee Groups, by Region

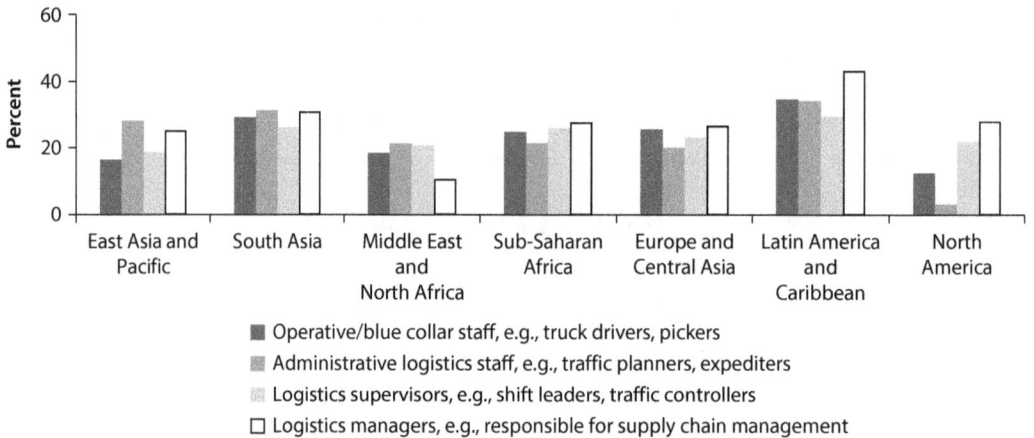

■ Operative/blue collar staff, e.g., truck drivers, pickers
▒ Administrative logistics staff, e.g., traffic planners, expediters
░ Logistics supervisors, e.g., shift leaders, traffic controllers
☐ Logistics managers, e.g., responsible for supply chain management

Source: Logistics Performance Index 2016.

groups (operative, administrative and supervisory), about a third of respondents indicated low or very low availability of staff.

Comparatively high staff shortages of between 20 percent and 30 percent at all job levels were reported in South Asia and Sub-Saharan Africa. The picture is more nuanced in East Asia and Pacific, were shortages of administrative and managerial staff were more acute than those of operative and supervisory staff. In the Middle East and North Africa, the low level of staff shortage at the managerial level (11 percent) vs. the other levels (around 20 percent each) stands out. This could be a favorable outcome of higher education programs (B.Sc. and

Figure E.3   Respondents Indicating "Low" or "Very Low" Availability of Qualified Personnel in the Respective Employee Groups, by Income Group

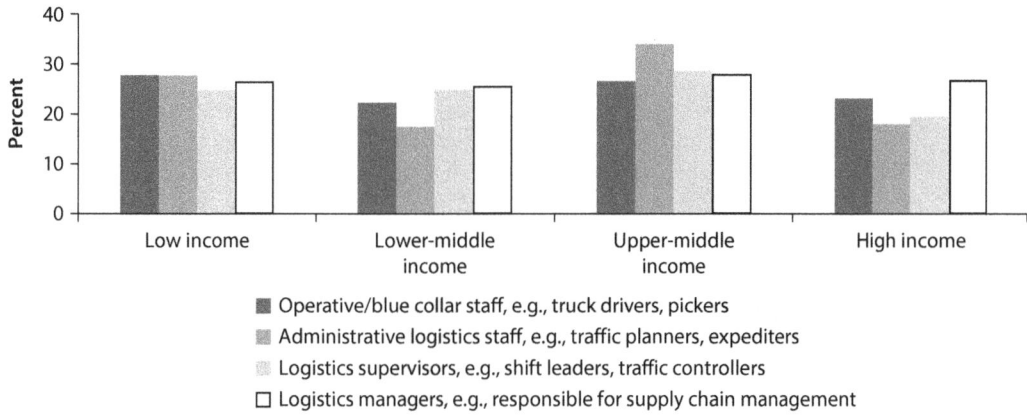

Source: Logistics Performance Index 2016.

M.Sc.) in logistics and supply chain management that were introduced in the region over the past decade. Morocco could serve as an example of a country that owing to those programs does not see a severe shortage of managerial staff. However, difficulties in finding workers on lower sophistication levels, for example, truck drivers and warehouse pickers, are still pertinent in the country.

An interesting finding is that the severity of skills shortages varies much less by income group (low, lower middle, upper middle and high income) than by LPI quintile, where a clear divide can be seen between the first and second quintile on the one hand and the remaining, higher performing ones, on the other hand. No clear picture emerges when comparing skills shortages by income group. The shortage of logistics managers for instance is perceived as equally high in the lowest income group (26 percent) as in the highest one (27 percent). Larger differences can only be spotted among the availability of administrative logistics staff, which is fairly abundant in high and lower middle income countries (with a shortage of only 17–18 percent), and a comparative scarcity in upper middle income countries (with a shortage of 34 percent).

Note

1. 1st LPI quintile = countries with the lowest overall 2016 LPI score; 5th LPI quintile = countries with the highest overall 2016 LPI score.

Environmental Benefits Statement

The World Bank Group is committed to reducing its environmental footprint. In support of this commitment, we leverage electronic publishing options and print-on-demand technology, which is located in regional hubs worldwide. Together, these initiatives enable print runs to be lowered and shipping distances decreased, resulting in reduced paper consumption, chemical use, greenhouse gas emissions, and waste.

We follow the recommended standards for paper use set by the Green Press Initiative. The majority of our books are printed on Forest Stewardship Council (FSC)–certified paper, with nearly all containing 50–100 percent recycled content. The recycled fiber in our book paper is either unbleached or bleached using totally chlorine-free (TCF), processed chlorine–free (PCF), or enhanced elemental chlorine–free (EECF) processes.

More information about the Bank's environmental philosophy can be found at http://www.worldbank.org/corporateresponsibility.

green
press
INITIATIVE

www.ingramcontent.com/pod-product-compliance
Lightning Source LLC
Chambersburg PA
CBHW082106210326
41599CB00033B/6606